Becoming God Duo

The Power of Marriage and Ministry

Karen Pless Gaines

DEDICATION

This book is dedicated to all couples seeking a deeper relationship with God and each other. It highlights the power of faith in navigating the ups and downs of marriage. To those who have shared their wisdom and experience, and those just starting their journey, we hope this work offers hope, encouragement, and inspiration.

We express our heartfelt gratitude to couples who exemplify the beauty and strength of faith-filled partnerships. Their commitment shows the transformative power of a God-centered marriage, guiding others along the way. Your love and dedication reflect God's grace and the joy of living for Him.

Additionally, this book is for couples facing daily challenges as they work to build a strong, God-centered marriage. We understand the struggles and sacrifices involved in nurturing this bond, and we hope these reflections remind you of God's constant presence. You are not alone, and even in difficult times, His love remains. May these pages bring comfort and inspiration, helping you cultivate a marriage filled with God's love and grace.

CONTENTS

INTRODUCTION

Let's face it—marriage isn't always a walk in the park. I've learned this lesson the hard way more times than I'd like to admit. But through the challenges, I've come to appreciate the couples who have faced storms together and emerged stronger. These are the people I look to for inspiration; they bear their battle scars proudly and offer wisdom that comes from years of commitment and resilience. One piece of advice consistently rings true among them: God must be at the center of your marriage.

It's easy to be kind and loving to those outside our home, yet sometimes we neglect to show that same grace to our spouse. Have you ever found yourself being more patient with a stranger than with the person you share your life with? It's a wake-up call—unity within marriage is crucial, and that unity must include God. After all, He is the ultimate source of love, forgiveness, and empathy, and we're called to reflect that in our relationships.

A few years back, I found myself at a crossroads in my marriage, grappling with feelings of hurt and disappointment. My spouse had done some things that left me feeling wounded, and trying to communicate felt almost impossible. I remember a particularly moments when he would brush past me, and I would instinctively flinch away from his touch. It was as if a wall had formed between us, and I was desperate for answers.

In my quiet moments of prayer, I sought God's guidance, asking Him how I could mend the rift in our relationship. Then one evening, something profound happened. In one of those moments when I flinched away from him, I heard in my spirit.: "Woman, heal thyself." It struck me like lightning because I recognized it as a reference to the words that Jesus spoke, "Physician, heal thyself." Intrigued, I explored its meaning further and discovered a powerful truth: Before attempting to correct others, make sure you aren't guilty of the same fault.

It was a revelation! I realized that I couldn't expect my husband to change if I continued to mirror his hurtful actions. If I truly wanted to foster change, I had to shift the way I responded to him. It's so easy to get caught up in the pain we feel and to mirror that hurt back to our partner. But that's not the path to healing, especially in a marriage.

It's so easy to get caught up in the pain of our experiences, retaliating in frustration instead of seeking understanding. But that's not the path we should choose, especially when it comes to our spouse. Instead, we must approach each other with love and a willingness to heal. This journey of self-discovery and growth became my guiding light, reminding me that healing begins within.

As you read this book and embark on your own journey to understand what it means to be a unified couple under God, I want to set the record straight. This isn't just a message for women; it's for every couple striving to grow together in faith. Marriage is not merely a contract between two individuals; it's a spiritual journey designed by God, meant to create a beautiful tapestry of partnership and love.

Here are a few key points to consider as you navigate your own marriage:

1. **Make God Your Foundation**

If you want a strong marriage, start by inviting God into your relationship. Pray together, study scripture, and seek His guidance in your decisions. When God is at the center, you'll find the strength to overcome obstacles and the wisdom to navigate life's challenges together.

2. **Practice Empathy and Forgiveness**

In the heat of the moment, it can be all too easy to forget the compassion we extend to others. Remember, your spouse is human too—flaws and all. Acknowledge their feelings, be willing to forgive, and strive to understand their perspective. Cultivating a spirit of empathy will deepen your bond and strengthen your connection.

3. **Prioritize Unity**

Every good marriage thrives on unity. It's essential to pull together as a team, especially during tough times. Share your dreams, goals, and concerns openly. This sense of togetherness will not only help you face challenges but also celebrate triumphs side by side.

4. **Seek Help When Needed**

It's important to recognize that if you're in an abusive relationship, that is not what God intends for you. He doesn't condone harmful behavior. If you find yourself in such a situation, please seek help. You deserve to be treated with love and respect, and there are resources available to assist you.

As we embark on this journey of exploration together, let's remember that marriage is more than just a bond; it's a spiritual adventure. Let's encourage one another to grow in faith and love, becoming that beautiful duo God designed us to be. Here's to thriving together, grounded in God's love! I pray this book helps you on your journey.

You will find discussion questions for each chapter in the back of this book. I encourage you to take time to sit with your spouse and use these questions as a guide for open discussion on each of these areas of the relationship.

CHAPTER 1

UNDERSTANDING GOD'S DESIGN FOR MARRIAGE

From the very dawn of creation, God established the institution of marriage, not as a mere societal construct, but as a sacred covenant reflecting His own divine nature. Genesis 2:24 beautifully articulates this foundational truth: "Therefore a man shall leave his father and his mother and hold fast to his wife, and they shall become one flesh." This isn't merely a statement about physical union; it's a profound declaration of spiritual oneness, a partnership designed to reflect the intimate relationship between Christ and His Church. This union, ordained by God, transcends cultural norms and societal trends; it stands as a timeless testament to His love and design.

The concept of "one flesh" speaks to a level of unity far exceeding mere companionship. It encompasses emotional, intellectual, and spiritual interconnectedness, a deep-seated bond that withstands the storms of life. This oneness is not about the erasure of individual identities, but rather a beautiful blending of two unique souls into a unified whole, each complementing and enriching the other. Think of a stunning tapestry – each thread distinct, yet woven together to create a masterpiece of breathtaking beauty. That, in essence, is the core of God's design for marriage.

Throughout scripture, we find examples of marital relationships that, while imperfect, offer valuable insights into the divine blueprint. Adam and Eve, despite their tragic fall, represent the initial ideal – a partnership created in God's image, reflecting His love and harmony. While their story highlights the devastating consequences of disobedience, it also underscores the enduring nature of God's love and His unwavering commitment to His creation.

Consider the relationship of Abraham and Sarah, a testament to faith, patience, and unwavering commitment. Their journey, filled with both blessings and trials, showcases the importance of mutual trust and reliance on God's guidance. Their story exemplifies the challenges and triumphs inherent in a God-centered marriage, reminding us that faith is not a shield against hardship, but rather a source of strength and resilience in the face of adversity.

The Old Testament prophets often employed marital metaphors to illustrate God's covenant relationship with His people. Hosea's marriage, marked by infidelity and reconciliation, serves as a powerful allegory of God's relentless love and unwavering faithfulness towards His chosen people, even in the face of their repeated disobedience. This illustrates the transformative power of grace and forgiveness within a marriage, mirroring the boundless grace offered by God Himself.

The New Testament, too, speaks profoundly to the sacredness of marriage. Jesus Himself, attending a wedding in Cana, elevates the institution to a level of celebration and sanctification. He affirms the union as a sacred bond, reflecting the union between Christ and the Church, a relationship characterized by love, sacrifice, and unending devotion. Ephesians 5:22-33 beautifully describes this relationship, calling husbands to love their wives as Christ loved the Church and wives to submit to their husbands in reverence and respect. This is not a call for subjugation, but rather a call for mutual submission, reflecting the complementary roles within a loving partnership.

Understanding the roles of husband and wife within this design requires a careful examination of scripture. The call for submission is not a call for inferiority, but rather a mutual yielding to one another, a recognition of each other's strengths and weaknesses, and a willingness to put the other's needs before one's own. This requires a delicate balance – a partnership built on equality, where each partner respects and values the other's unique contributions and gifts. It's not about dominance or control, but about mutual support, encouragement, and selfless love.

God's design emphasizes partnership and equality, not hierarchy. Husbands are called to lead with love, not authority; to serve, not to dominate. Wives are called to respect and honor their husbands, not to be subservient. The ideal is a unity of purpose, a harmonious blending of strengths and weaknesses, where each partner empowers and uplifts the other. This calls for open communication, mutual understanding, and a willingness to yield to the other's needs.

The concept of covenant is central to understanding God's design for marriage. A covenant is not merely an agreement; it's a solemn vow, a sacred promise made before God. It represents a lifelong commitment, a pledge of unwavering loyalty and faithfulness, regardless of circumstances. It's a commitment that endures through joy and sorrow, through prosperity and hardship, a commitment that transcends the ever-changing tides of human emotion. This covenant reflects God's own covenant with His people, a testament to His steadfast love and faithfulness.

Furthermore, the understanding of God's design for marriage extends beyond the confines of the marital relationship itself. It influences every facet of a couple's life, from their spiritual practices to their interactions with family and friends. It shapes their decisions, their actions, and their overall worldview. A God-centered marriage is not just a personal relationship; it's a powerful testament to the transformative power of faith, a beacon of hope and inspiration to those around them.

It's important to note that no marriage is perfect. Every couple faces challenges, struggles, and periods of doubt. However, a God-centered marriage is not defined by the absence of conflict, but by the way couples navigate these challenges through faith, prayer, and mutual support. It's a relationship sustained by grace, forgiveness, and a shared commitment to grow in love and understanding.

The biblical examples we've explored reveal both the ideal and the reality of marriage. They are not perfect models, but rather relatable narratives offering valuable lessons. They show us that God's design is not a rigid formula but a flexible framework, allowing for individual personalities, unique circumstances, and the unpredictable twists and turns of life. What remains constant is the foundational principles – love, commitment, mutual respect, and a steadfast reliance on God's grace and guidance. This enduring foundation, built upon the rock of faith, enables marriages to withstand the storms and to thrive amidst the challenges.

Ultimately, understanding God's design for marriage is a journey, a continuous process of learning, growing, and adapting. It's about striving towards an ideal, recognizing our imperfections, and relying on God's grace to guide us along the path. It's about embracing the challenges, celebrating the joys, and never losing sight of the sacred covenant we have made, both with each other and with God. It is a journey of unwavering faith, mutual love, and unending devotion – a journey that reflects the very heart of God. It's a journey worth taking, a journey that leads to a life of deeper intimacy, richer purpose, and profound spiritual growth, not just individually, but together, as one flesh, reflecting the beautiful image of God.

Prayer: The Heartbeat of Your Marriage

The moment you hear the word "prayer," doesn't it conjure up images of quiet reflection and an intimate connection with something greater than ourselves? In a God-centered marriage, prayer is not just an individual endeavor; it's the very heartbeat of your relationship. It's that sacred time where two people come together, sharing their deepest worries and lifting each other up while trusting in a loving Father.

But let's clarify: building a prayerful partnership isn't merely about repeating the same phrases or ticking boxes on a religious checklist. It's about crafting a genuine connection with God together. Imagine turning your individual faith into a joint experience of worship— something powerful and deeply loving. When you pray together, conflicts can turn into moments of grace, and challenges morph into opportunities for growth.

Think about the deeper level of connection you experience when you kneel together in prayer. In this intimate act, vulnerability blossoms. Fears are confessed, hearts are bared, and a unique bond is forged. This shared vulnerability cultivates a foundation of trust that can weather any storm life throws your way.

Picture it as a sacred conversation between two souls and their Creator. It's not just about asking for blessings or begging for relief; it's about mutual dependence and trust in God's grace. In this dialogue, unspoken feelings are acknowledged, and hopes are nurtured in faith. Together, you create a beautiful rhythm that reverberates through the everyday journey of life.

Consider a couple facing a daunting financial hurdle. Instead of giving in to anxiety and fear, they turn to prayer, sharing their thoughts and concerns with each other and God. Through this simple act, their fear transforms into trust, their anxiety into hope, and their worries into faith. They don't just face the challenge; they grow closer to each other and God, turning what could have been a conflict into a profound catalyst for unity.

Incorporating prayer into your daily lives doesn't have to be grandiose. It begins with small, meaningful acts—perhaps a shared prayer before meals, a quiet moment of reflection before sleep, or a simple acknowledgment of God's presence throughout your day. These small moments add up, creating a rich tapestry of faith woven into the fabric of your relationship.

Kick things off with a sincere, simple prayer. No need for fancy rhetoric or intricate theology—just speak from your hearts. Express gratitude for the blessings you share, acknowledge your shortcomings, and share your dreams and worries for your life together. Ask for guidance, strength, and wisdom as you navigate the beautiful journey of marriage.

Disagreements are bound to happen in any relationship. Whether it's a heated argument or just a misunderstanding, these challenges are part of life. But in a prayerful partnership, you learn to see these moments not as obstacles, but as opportunities to deepen your connection with one another and with God. Prayer provides clarity and opens up channels of understanding, enabling you to work through conflict and embrace forgiveness and peace.

Imagine a couple on the brink of a serious disagreement, feeling like their relationship is hanging by a thread. Instead of succumbing to anger or silence, they decide to pray together. They ask for the wisdom to see things from each other's perspectives, for the grace to release past mistakes, and for the strength to tackle their issues as a united front. Through prayer, they don't just seek answers; they acknowledge their imperfections and commit to growing together. Surprisingly, this brings them back to a place of understanding, rebuilding their bond even stronger than before.

Remember, prayer isn't a magic wand that solves every problem instantly; it's a powerful tool that helps couples navigate their challenges with grace and understanding. It's a way to seek God's wisdom, embrace vulnerability, and find a path toward forgiveness. In the midst of conflict, prayer becomes a lifeline—a shared act of faith that binds you together, reminding you of your commitment to one another and to God. Embrace it, and watch how it transforms your marriage.

Imagine a marriage where prayer is at the heart of every decision, every challenge, and every moment of joy. Envision a couple facing life's ups and downs, hand in hand, finding strength and comfort in their faith together. Intercessory prayer in a marriage isn't just an act; it's a lifeline, a force that deepens intimacy and solidifies the bond of love. When one partner encounters trials, the other rises to the occasion, supporting them through heartfelt prayers that intertwine their souls and reinforce their commitment to one another.

Think about the transformative power of praying together—it's like setting the rhythm for a beautiful dance of faith and devotion that influences every aspect of life as a couple. This practice serves not only as a ritual but as the very heartbeat of the relationship, creating a shared journey that enhances intimacy and unity. It's a pilgrimage of love, guiding both partners toward spiritual maturity while drawing them closer to God and to each other.

There will be moments when praying feels challenging. Perhaps the words don't come easily, or faith wavers under the weight of life's pressures. Yet, even in those vulnerable times, simply seeking God together can profoundly strengthen the connection between partners. It's through these struggles that faith is fortified, love blossoms, and the light of devotion shines brighter than ever.

Through this sacred act of prayer, couples not only cultivate a stronger marriage but also embark on a journey toward a deeper relationship with God, discovering an unshakeable sense of peace, purpose, and joy. Amidst life's storms, that shared prayer becomes an anchor, a safe harbor, offering unwavering strength and comfort. It's during these serene moments of communion that renewal occurs, and a deeper purpose in shared life is revealed.

Consider a couple navigating a crucial decision—whether to change careers, relocate, or embrace a significant life transition. Instead of relying solely on their thoughts or succumbing to outside pressures, they turn to prayer, seeking God's wisdom and guidance. Through this process, they clarify their vision and discover the courage to make choices aligned with God's plan, emboldening their faith and reinforcing their unity.

At its core, a prayerful partnership is about nurturing a deep, abiding relationship with God as a couple, allowing shared faith to seep into every corner of their lives. It's about creating a sacred space for vulnerability and honesty, where love can flourish on the fertile ground of devotion. By acknowledging their dependence on God's grace and seeking His guidance, they navigate their journey through life hand-in-hand, transforming their marriage into a powerful testament to the transformative power of faith, igniting hope, and shining as a beacon of light to those around them.

So, embark on this journey together—allow prayer to become the foundation of your marriage. Discover the profound intimacy and connection that awaits you. As you pray, you'll not only strengthen your relationship with each other but also experience the boundless love and grace of God, turning everyday moments into powerful testimonies of faith.

Forgiveness and Grace

Forgiveness. Just say the word, and it seems to echo with the promise of release, like shedding heavy burdens and setting your soul free. In a God-centered marriage, forgiveness is more than a kind gesture; it's a sacred responsibility, reflecting God's infinite grace and serving as the backbone of a lasting partnership. It's about the commitment to let go of past offenses, embrace reconciliation, and choose love over resentment time and time again. Each act of forgiveness is a conscious choice to mirror God's mercy, extending compassion and understanding even when it's toughest.

The Bible offers profound insights on this journey of forgiveness, painting it as a badge of strength rather than a sign of weakness—a true marker of spiritual maturity. Take, for instance, the parable of the unforgiving servant in Matthew 18. This gripping story reveals the harsh reality that the servant, who received enormous forgiveness from his master, faced dire consequences for withholding the same mercy from another. It drives home a powerful truth: we cannot fully experience God's grace unless we're willing to pay it forward, offering forgiveness to those around us.

In marriage, this principle gains even more weight. Conflicts, disagreements, and even betrayals are part of the human experience; they will emerge. Every relationship is tested by the pressures of daily life, the intricacies of individual personalities, and the reality of human imperfection. However, what distinguishes a God-centered marriage is the proactive choice to navigate these conflicts through the lens of forgiveness. It's a bold, intentional commitment to grace, a decision to prioritize healing over harboring old wounds.

Think of resentment as a slow-acting poison, quietly eroding the foundation of your relationship. It seeps into your heart, fueling anger and creating walls between you and your partner. You might notice it showing up through withdrawn affections, silence that feels like a chasm, or cutting remarks that sting. Ultimately, it suffocates love and squashes intimacy, leaving you feeling isolated. On the flip side, forgiveness is like a healing balm; it soothes wounds and repairs the fractures between you. It doesn't mean you condone hurtful behavior; it signifies the power to release anger and pain, opening the door to a healthier future grounded in grace and understanding.

So, how do you cultivate this vital virtue of forgiveness in your marriage? It's not a one-off moment; it's a continuous practice, a conscious choice you make every day. To embody forgiveness, you must embrace humility, engage in self-reflection, and be willing to confront your own shortcomings. Empathy is essential; it allows you to step into your partner's shoes, acknowledging their pain and motivations.

Start by prompting honest self-reflection. Before diving into any confrontation, ask yourself: What role did I play in this situation? What were my motivations? Where could I have done better? Recognizing your own part is crucial; it diffuses anger and fosters humility. This practice opens the door for genuine dialogue and mutual understanding—a crucial step in moving forward together.

Next up is open, heartfelt communication. Create a safe space where both of you feel free to share your emotions without fear of judgment. Express your hurt, disappointment, or anger respectfully and compassionately. Don't forget to listen deeply to your partner's perspective—seek to understand their feelings, even if you don't fully agree. Remember, the goal isn't to win the argument but to connect deeply with one another.

Then comes the most transformative step: actively choosing forgiveness. This might be the hardest part, but its impact is profound. Forgiveness isn't about forgetting; it's about letting go of the grip resentment has on you. It's a deliberate decision to step out of the cycle of hurt and anger, extending grace and prioritizing the health of your relationship. You may find that it takes time—sometimes multiple acts of forgiveness—to truly release the past. Every effort you make counts.

And always remember, forgiveness doesn't nullify the offense's severity. It doesn't excuse wrongdoing; instead, it liberates you from resentment's hold, allowing you to move forward and rebuild trust. Think of it as an act of faith—a beautiful testament to the strength and resilience of your love.

Consider a couple grappling with the aftermath of infidelity: the pain is profound, and the sense of betrayal is overwhelming. Yet, in a God-centered marriage, forgiveness becomes a beacon of hope, guiding the way to healing and restoration. It's a challenging journey, demanding vulnerability, open communication, and a steadfast commitment to rebuilding trust. This process involves confronting the hurt and acknowledging each other's pain, holding tight to the belief that love, rooted in forgiveness, can rise above even the toughest trials. Embrace the journey—it's worth every step you take together.

Forgiveness is more than just an act; it's a profound spiritual journey that mirrors the boundless mercy and grace that God extends to us. Imagine standing at a crossroads where humility, patience, and unwavering faith become your guiding lights. This journey challenges you to release the weight of the past and to step boldly into a future brimming with hope and healing. Remember, amidst the chaos of pain and struggle, that God's grace is enough. His love is enduring, and His transformative power to heal knows no limits.

Let's delve into the concept of grace—God's unmerited favor that shines through even in our imperfections. In a God-centered marriage, grace is the lens through which we choose to see our partner. Each flaw and failing becomes an opportunity to extend kindness, not because they've earned it, but because we, too, are in constant need of grace. We're called to reflect that divine grace in how we relate to one another.

Picture this: one partner frequently forgets special dates or makes careless mistakes. Instead of reacting with frustration, the other partner chooses to embrace grace. They recognize that everyone has flaws, including themselves, and they respond with compassion rather than criticism. This doesn't mean turning a blind eye to unacceptable behavior; instead, it's an invitation to connect deeply, addressing the root issues with empathy and patience. The result? A relationship that flourishes with understanding, mutual support, and an unwavering love that can weather any storm.

Cultivating forgiveness and grace is a lifelong endeavor—a continuous refining of the heart and soul. It's all about making a heartfelt commitment to release compassion and understanding, even when disappointment looms large. By striving to reflect God's incredible mercy, we embrace the reality that we are all imperfect beings, desperately in need of His love. This journey of forgiveness and grace becomes a powerful testament to the transformative power of faith, linking hearts in a bond that's strong, resilient, and deeply reflective of God's unwavering love.

As you embark on this shared spiritual path, recognize that it's not just about strengthening your marriage; it's about deepening your connection with God and with each other. This beautiful union—built on love, faith, and an unwavering commitment to the divine—becomes a continuous pilgrimage. Your journey through forgiveness and grace speaks volumes about the enduring power of love, revealing the immense beauty that lies in embracing the transformative possibilities that await. Embrace this adventure, and watch how it nurtures your relationship into something truly divine.

The Power of Communication

Imagine a vibrant garden—a place where blossoms flourish, colors burst forth, and life thrives. This idyllic scene isn't just a testament to nature; it's an analogy for what makes a marriage truly blossom: consistent, open, and honest communication. Just as a garden requires sunlight, water, and dedicated care, a relationship anchored in faith needs effective communication to sustain its vitality. Without it, the strongest love can wither under miscommunication, unspoken needs, and unresolved conflicts.

In a God-centered marriage, communication becomes a sacred act. It serves as a mirror reflecting our relationship with God and a bridge to deeper intimacy with our partner. Think of it as the very oxygen that fuels your connection. When we neglect this essential part of our relationship, we risk letting misunderstandings fester like weeds, choking out the love and joy we've cultivated.

So, what does this look like in practice? The foundation of effective communication lies in active listening. This means more than just hearing the words our spouse shares; it's about truly grasping their emotions, perspectives, and needs. It calls for us to put our thoughts on hold, to fully engage with our partner, and to listen with empathy and compassion. It's about tuning into the unspoken language—the body language, tone of voice, and facial expressions that often convey feelings words cannot.

Just as gardeners meticulously tend to their plants, we must nurture our relationship. Address conflicts early, weed out resentment, and nurture the growth of mutual understanding. The simple act of sharing and listening can transform your bond into a haven of support and love.

Remember, in your marriage garden, silence, avoidance, and passive-aggressive behavior will only lead to a tangled mess. But when we nurture open communication, we allow the sun and rain of understanding and compassion to create a thriving landscape of love. By cultivating your gardens together, you are fostering an environment where both partners can bloom beautifully.

Think back to a time when you really felt heard and understood. You know that warm feeling of being totally seen and accepted? That's what active listening is all about. It's about creating a space where both you and your partner can share what's on your mind without worrying about being judged.

If you want to up your active listening game, try a couple of easy tricks. First, when your spouse is talking, try summarizing what they've said or putting it in your own words. It shows that you're really paying attention and gives them a chance to clear up any confusion.

Another helpful trick is to reflect back their emotions. Recognizing how they feel can go a long way—even if you don't totally see things their way. You might say something like, "It sounds like you're feeling pretty hurt and frustrated," or "I can tell you're feeling overwhelmed." Acknowledging those feelings can create a real sense of connection and understanding between you two. Just remember, it's all about being there for each other and strengthening that bond!

Effective communication in a marriage is like the glue that holds everything together, and at the heart of this glue is empathy. Imagine being able to step right into your spouse's shoes, seeing the world through their eyes. It's not just about hearing what they say, but truly understanding their feelings, even if you don't see eye to eye. That's the power of empathy! It can transform your relationship, allowing you to connect on a deeper level filled with compassion, understanding, and mutual respect.

But let's clear something up—empathy and sympathy aren't the same thing. Sympathy is feeling sorry for someone, while empathy goes a step further. It's about sharing in their feelings, being there alongside them, and truly understanding their perspective. In a God-centered marriage, empathy is not just important; it's essential. It helps us respond to our spouse's needs with kindness instead of defensiveness, creating a space where both partners feel supported and loved.

Now, let's talk about expressing needs and emotions. Many conflicts in relationships stem from unvoiced feelings or unclear communication. Often, it's not a lack of love, but rather a breakdown in communication that leads to misunderstandings. That's where "I" statements come into play. Instead of pointing fingers and saying things like, "You always leave your clothes on the floor," try rephrasing it: "I feel frustrated when I see clothes on the floor because it makes me feel like the house is messy." This way, you're focusing on your feelings rather than making accusations, paving the way for more constructive and engaging conversations. By fostering empathy and clear expression, you'll not only strengthen your relationship but also create a loving environment where both partners can thrive.

In a God-centered marriage, talking about our spiritual needs can really bring us closer together. Think about the moments when you share your struggles, prayer requests, or even the little victories in your faith journey—those are the times that strengthen your bond. Whether it's discussing a favorite Bible verse or just chatting about how faith plays into everyday life, these conversations are key. Plus, praying together isn't just a routine; it's a really special way to connect.

Of course, open communication isn't always easy. Life throws some challenges our way—past hurts, unresolved conflicts, and sometimes just different ways of expressing ourselves can make it tough to really talk things through. You know how it is: when we feel criticized, our first reaction is often to get the defensive, which can turn a small disagreement into a full-blown argument.

So how do we get past that? It's all about taking a step back and really listening. Instead of immediately jumping in to defend yourself, try to hear where your spouse is coming from. By focusing on understanding their feelings and showing empathy, we can address the real concerns and have those heart-to-heart conversations we all crave. At the end of the day, it's all about creating that space for honest talk and growth. Sure, it takes some effort, but the deeper connection we build is totally worth it!

Relationships can be a beautiful journey, but they also come with their own challenges, one of which is stonewalling. Imagine this: one partner becomes emotionally closed off, refusing to engage in conversation. This often happens when they feel overwhelmed, unheard, or criticized. To break through this barrier, it's essential to create a safe space for each other—a haven where both partners can express their thoughts and feelings without the fear of being judged or attacked.

Taking a pause when emotions run high isn't a sign of avoidance; it's actually a smart strategy to help foster meaningful dialogue. Don't underestimate the power of a moment to regroup and calm down—it can lead to more fruitful conversations.

Differing communication styles can also present a challenge. Some people communicate directly and assertively, while others may be more indirect or passive. Understanding these different styles is crucial for any couple. If your partner tends to be more reserved, try tuning in to those subtle hints and asking clarifying questions to delve deeper. Conversely, if your partner speaks their mind clearly, practice receiving their messages without taking them personally.

Emotional intelligence—or the lack thereof—can also play a significant role in how couples connect and communicate. Some individuals are naturally more in tune with their emotions and articulate, while others may struggle. Creating an environment where both of you can express yourselves freely is super important. Consider doing some activities or even a retreat to help boost that emotional understanding—it can really strengthen your connection.

In a marriage rooted in faith, communication transforms into something truly beautiful. It's so much more than just sharing facts; it's an opportunity to forge a profound connection not only with each other but also with God. Imagine the strength of a relationship that grows as you practice active listening and empathy, opening up about your feelings with honesty. This kind of vulnerability allows you to cultivate a love that truly embodies the grace of God.

So, let's celebrate the adventure of open communication! With a sprinkle of effort and some shared moments of spiritual growth, you can build a relationship that not only withstands the tests of time but also reflects the everlasting love God has for us. Embrace this journey together, and watch your bond flourish!

CHAPTER 2

NAVIGATING CHALLENGES WITH FAITH

The heart of any strong relationship—especially one grounded in faith—is about having each other's backs. It's not just about jumping in when things get tough; it's about really caring for each other's well-being, both in spirit and in everyday life. In a marriage centered on God, this support takes on a special meaning; it's like a reflection of the endless love and grace God gives us.

Think of your relationship as a back-and-forth exchange, where encouragement and selfless acts go hand in hand. It's about cheering each other on during the big wins and little victories, being there to lend a shoulder when things get rough, and providing strength when one of you feels worn out. This isn't a passive deal; it's all about making the effort to put your partner's needs and dreams front and center, even if it means delaying your own wants sometimes. It's not about ignoring your own needs but finding joy in helping your partner grow and thrive. However, this is not one-sided. This is not done through greed of one supporting the other and one that receives. This is a back and forth sharing of support.

Remember, that one of the ways to show that support is praying with and for each other. Whether it's taking a quiet moment together before dinner or spending time in deeper prayer, it brings you closer. Praying together creates a special bond, helping each of you grow spiritually while recognizing that you rely on God's strength together. When you pray for your spouse—hoping for their needs and dreams—you're jumping into their spiritual journey alongside them. It's an incredible way to connect not just with each other but also with God, making your relationship even stronger!

Imagine the power of sharing your personal struggles with your spouse. Remember that vulnerability isn't a sign of weakness; it's a bold act of courage that deepens your bond. When you open up about your fears, doubts, and shortcomings, you create a safe space for honesty and authenticity—an invitation for deeper intimacy and understanding.

Think about those moments of spiritual struggle—times of doubt, dryness, or wrestling with temptation. By sharing these experiences, you can lean on each other for strength and encouragement, mirroring the compassionate grace that God offers us continually. Embracing these discussions not only strengthens your relationship but also nurtures your individual growth.

But it doesn't stop there! Active participation in each other's lives is essential. Attend important events together, celebrate each milestone, and be there for one another during tough times. It's about being present, not just in body but with your heart and mind fully engaged. Listen intently when your partner shares their dreams and anxieties, offer encouragement, and lend a helping hand. Creating this supportive atmosphere ensures both partners feel deeply valued and cherished.

And let's not forget the daily grind! Though it may seem mundane, mutual support in everyday life—like tackling household chores together or cheering each other on in career ambitions—can profoundly impact your bond. When you share responsibilities, no matter how big or small, you foster a sense of teamwork that solidifies your partnership and commitment to each other's well-being.

Supporting each other's personal goals is another corner stone of a thriving relationship. Celebrate your spouse's achievements and stand by them during setbacks. Whether it's helping with research, providing emotional support, or simply being a sounding board, creating an environment where both partners feel empowered to chase their passions enriches the marriage. Remember, your partner's successes are intertwined with your own, and their growth elevates your relationship as a whole. You two have become one in Christ. So when one wins—so does the other.

Lastly, shared spiritual practices can be a wonderful way to cultivate your connection. Engage in regular prayer, Bible study, or church activities together. These shared experiences foster a sense of purpose and deepen your spiritual bond. Learning and growing together on this journey not only enriches your faith but also nurtures an intimacy that connects you on a soul level. A divided house can't stand, but united, you can overcome anything life throws at you.

So, embrace vulnerability, actively participate in each other's lives, support one another, and engage in shared spiritual practices. Together, you can build a beautiful, God-centered marriage that thrives on love, understanding, and mutual growth.

Building a thriving, God-centered marriage is an enriching journey that calls for intentional effort and shared experiences. One of the most effective ways to deepen your connection is by dedicating time to spiritual disciplines together. Imagine setting aside special moments to read Scripture, meditate on a meaningful passage, or engage in heartfelt prayer. These shared moments not only foster intimacy but also deepen your understanding of God's word, creating a sanctuary of encouragement and growth. Rotating the leadership of these sessions allows each partner to bring their unique insights and spiritual gifts to the table, enriching the experience for both of you.

Mutual support also thrives on celebrating each other's strengths and recognizing the unique gifts that each partner brings into the relationship. In a God-centered marriage, we understand that we are beautifully made with distinct talents that complement each other. Taking the time to celebrate these gifts creates a nurturing atmosphere where both partners feel valued and cherished. It's a beautiful acknowledgment of the diversity within your relationship, strengthening your bond with mutual respect and admiration.

Constructive feedback is another vital pillar of support. It's essential to remember that this isn't about criticism or judgment; rather, it's about offering loving advice aimed at helping your spouse grow. When delivering feedback, focus on the behavior instead of the person. This approach creates a safe space for improvement, free from defensiveness or resentment. Framing your feedback with love, empathy, and understanding reinforces the goal of mutual growth and fosters an atmosphere of encouragement.

Forgiveness is perhaps one of the most crucial components in a healthy, God-centered marriage. Rooted in Christ's unconditional love, forgiveness is not a sign of weakness but rather a courageous act of love and grace. Holding onto resentment only creates walls that block intimacy and support. Choosing to forgive each other regularly—releasing bitterness and anger—paves the way for healing and reconciliation, allowing your relationship to flourish. Remember, forgiveness isn't about condoning missteps; it's about freeing yourself from the burden of resentment.

Another key to effective mutual support lies in understanding your spouse's love language. Each of us expresses and receives love in our unique ways—some through acts of service, others through words of affirmation, gifts, quality time, or physical touch. By taking the time to learn your partner's love language, you can tailor your expressions of support to meet their specific needs, ensuring that your gestures resonate deeply. This attentiveness not only strengthens your bond but also deepens the intimacy and support within your relationship.

In essence, mutual support and shared growth are the heartbeats of a flourishing, God-centered marriage. It's about the beautiful interplay of giving and receiving, encouragement and affirmation, and navigating life's ups and downs together. By prioritizing each other's spiritual and practical well-being and nurturing a shared faith, couples can build a partnership that embodies God's unwavering love and grace. Your journey together stands as a testament to the transformative power of selfless service, steadfast commitment, and a love that endures through life's trials. It's this mutual support that lays the groundwork for a strong, resilient marriage, echoing the never-failing love God has for His people. As you embark on this journey, embrace each other with open hearts, ready to grow, forgive, and celebrate the incredible adventure of love together.

Dealing with External Pressures

The sanctuary of our marriage, though built on the solid rock of faith, is not immune to the winds of external pressure. Just as a mighty oak withstands the fiercest storms, so too must our relationship endure the trials that arise from sources beyond our immediate control. Family disagreements, societal expectations, and the ever-present pull of worldly distractions can test the strength of even the most deeply rooted commitment. Navigating these external pressures requires a unified front, a shared understanding, and a constant reliance on the unwavering love and guidance of God.

One of the most common battlegrounds we encounter is the realm of family dynamics. Differing opinions on child- rearing, financial matters, or even seemingly insignificant details can create rifts between spouses and their respective families. The key to navigating these challenges lies in maintaining a united front. Before diving into discussions with family members, take time to discuss your perspectives, aligning your responses and presenting a united position. This doesn't mean suppressing individual opinions; rather, it involves finding common ground and expressing it as a collective decision. This shows respect for each other and presents a united, strong front to any external pressures. Avoid engaging in arguments or disagreements in front of family members, as this can exacerbate tensions and weaken your position. Instead, address conflicts privately and come out with a unified solution that fortifies your bond.

Furthermore, actively communicate your boundaries and expectations. It is essential to have frank discussions about the limits you're comfortable with in terms of family involvement in your lives. Openly communicating your boundaries prevents misunderstandings and protects the sanctity of your marriage from undue influence. For instance, if you prefer to make major financial decisions without family input, clearly communicate this to avoid conflict. Similarly, set limits on the level of involvement in your children's upbringing, ensuring everyone is on the same page. Respecting these boundaries, both within your family and with your spouse's family, is crucial for maintaining a healthy and harmonious relationship. A unified and clear communication fosters mutual understanding and minimizes potential conflicts.

But it's not just family pressures we face. Society often throws its weight around, trying to shape our perceptions of what a marriage should look like. The relentless barrage of media portrayals and cultural norms can subtly chip away at the heart of a faith-based union. That's why it's so important to reaffirm your values and beliefs continually. Carve out intentional time for prayer, dive into scripture together, and engage in activities that strengthen not just your relationship but also your spiritual connection. These shared moments of devotion become the bedrock of your commitment, equipping you both to stand resilient against the world's pressures.

Remember, your marriage is more than just a partnership; it's a sacred covenant that reflects your faith. It's a testament to the love and dedication you both share—a love that defies societal expectations. Embrace the journey together, knowing that as long as you stand united in faith and purpose, nothing from the outside can break the bonds you've built.

In today's fast-paced world, staying focused on what truly matters can feel like an uphill battle. The allure of chasing after wealth, climbing the corporate ladder, and accumulating material possessions often drowns out the vital essence of our marriages and the spiritual foundations that support them. So, how do we combat these worldly distractions? It starts with the commitment to create intentional space for your relationship!

In our busy lives, it's essential to carve out time for each other. How about scheduling regular date nights where you can escape the daily grind? These nights can be a wonderful opportunity for deep conversations and shared experiences that nurture your emotional and spiritual bond. Think of it as a reset button for your union; a time to reconnect and remind yourselves of the core values that brought you together. By prioritizing your relationship in this way, you're not just resisting external pressures—you're reinforcing the strength and significance of your partnership!

Yet, navigating the challenges outside of your relationship can sometimes require more than just your own efforts. Seeking help and support from trusted friends, family, or mentors who share your faith can make a world of difference. Imagine having a network of like-minded individuals cheering you on and lifting you up in tough times! Whether it's a wise pastor or a spiritual advisor, leaning on someone who can offer fresh insights can help you reaffirm your commitment to both each other and your faith. Remember, asking for help isn't a sign of weakness; it's a bold declaration of your dedication to building a stronger marriage rooted in love and faith.

And let's not forget one of the most powerful tools at our disposal—prayer. There's something truly transformative about coming together in prayer. It's an opportunity to communicate with God, seeking His guidance and strength. Through prayer, we can find the wisdom and patience to tackle any challenge that comes our way, feeling uplifted and united in our faith. It's a reminder that, no matter how tough things get, God's love is steadfast, and He gives us the strength to overcome obstacles together.

In the end, navigating external pressures in a faith-based marriage involves a proactive, united approach that fills your relationship with purpose. By fostering open communication, establishing clear boundaries, prioritizing your spiritual connection, and seeking support when needed, you can build a resilient partnership that thrives amid any storm life throws your way. Your unwavering faith, mutual love, and commitment to God act as an indestructible shield against adversity, showcasing the beauty of your marriage as a testament to His enduring love, grace, and mercy. Embrace your challenges with faith and witness the incredible, transformative power of God's love in your lives!

Financial Stewardship in Marriage

The foundation of any successful marriage rests on many pillars, but financial stability is a cornerstone often overlooked amidst discussions of love, faith, and commitment. While romantic gestures and heartfelt conversations are vital, a shared understanding and responsible management of finances can prevent considerable stress and conflict, paving the way for a more harmonious and fulfilling partnership. From a Christian perspective, financial stewardship is not merely about accumulating wealth; it's about using our resources wisely, responsibly, and in accordance with God's will, reflecting His abundant provision in our lives.

This journey of financial stewardship begins with open and honest communication. Before exchanging vows, couples should have frank discussions about their individual financial situations, including income, debts, spending habits, and financial goals. This isn't about scrutinizing each other's past mistakes but creating a shared understanding of the present landscape. Transparency builds trust, and trust forms the bedrock of a strong financial partnership. If one partner has significant debts, it's crucial to discuss a realistic plan for repayment, perhaps involving joint efforts or seeking professional financial guidance. Tackling these issues upfront prevents hidden resentments that can spring up later and threaten your bond.

Once a clear picture of the combined financial landscape emerges, creating a shared budget becomes paramount. This isn't about strict control or restricting individual spending; rather, it's about collaborative planning and responsible resource allocation. Sit down together, preferably with a cup of coffee and a calm demeanor, and discuss your monthly income, expenses, and savings goals. Allocate funds for necessities such as housing, food, transportation, and utilities, ensuring sufficient provisions for each area. Beyond the essentials, budget for discretionary spending, acknowledging that both partners need room for personal purchases and hobbies. The key is finding a balance that respects individual needs while ensuring fiscal responsibility.

Consider using budgeting tools or apps to simplify the process. There are plenty of free or affordable options that come equipped with features like expense tracking, budgeting categories, and savings goals to keep everything organized. Plus, these tools can reveal valuable insights into your spending habits, helping you identify areas where adjustments may be beneficial. And don't forget to review your budget regularly—monthly or quarterly catch-ups. This helps ensure your spending aligns with your goals while allowing you to adjust for those unexpected expenses that life often throws your way. Flexibility is crucial; your budget should be a living document that evolves with your circumstances.

In the landscape of our financial lives, saving stands as a cornerstone of stewardship, acting as a safeguard against the unexpected and laying the groundwork for long-term stability. Picture this: a joint savings account dedicated to emergencies, short-term dreams, and those lofty long-term aspirations you both share. Even if it starts as just a small percentage of your income each month, that consistent effort sends a powerful message: you're nurturing a culture of saving and building a secure future together.

Proverbs 21:20 resonates profoundly in this context, reminding us, "The wise store up choice food and olive oil, but fools gulp theirs down." It's not just about putting away money; it's about embracing the wisdom of planning for the future—an echo of God's wise and providential nature.

But financial stewardship doesn't stop with saving; it encompasses giving back to our communities as well. Tithing, the sacred practice of giving ten percent of your income to the church, is a beautiful tradition that reflects our commitment to supporting God's work and sharing our blessings. Beyond the tithe, consider regular giving to charities that resonate with your values. Imagine how fulfilling it feels to know your generosity is making a real difference! This act isn't merely about financial contributions—it's a declaration of faith, a reflection of divine grace, and a profound opportunity to foster humility and gratitude within your hearts.

Now, let's talk about debt management—an area that can feel daunting yet is essential for financial health. High levels of debt can cast a shadow over your plans and cause stress. If you find yourselves in this situation, don't despair! Develop a systematic approach to tackle it. Create a repayment schedule that prioritizes higher-interest debts first. Explore options like consolidation or financial counseling. Communication is key here; open discussions about debt foster mutual understanding and a collaborative approach to overcoming challenges. Remember, seeking professional financial advice is a proactive step, not a sign of failure.

Investing wisely is yet another dimension of responsible financial stewardship. Approach this with a thoughtful plan and consider consulting a financial advisor to guide you through the myriad of options—from low-risk savings accounts to higher-risk stocks and bonds. Every investment carries its own blend of potential returns and risks. Align your strategy with your unique goals, risk tolerance, and timeline. And always remember: investment involves risks, so approach each decision with prayerful consideration and a balanced perspective.

As you navigate your financial journey, keep in mind that it's a winding road filled with ups, downs, and unexpected turns. There will be expenses that catch you off guard and moments when you need to adjust your plans. What remains steadfast is your commitment to managing your finances in a way that honors God, strengthens your relationship, and secures your family's future. Regularly assess your financial health, celebrate your wins—big and small—and embrace the lessons learned from setbacks. Through heartfelt communication, shared responsibilities, and prayerful guidance, you can lay a strong financial foundation that nurtures a flourishing marriage rooted in faith.

Lastly, never underestimate the power of prayer and spiritual guidance on this journey. Pray together for wisdom and discernment in your financial decisions. Dive into scripture, reflecting on passages that touch on wealth, prosperity, and stewardship. Consider attending financial stewardship seminars or workshops offered by your church or other reputable organizations; these can provide not just insights, but also inspiration.

Remember, true wealth isn't found in material possessions but in the richness of your relationship with God and one another. Your marriage is a sacred covenant, a partnership blessed by God, and practicing responsible financial stewardship is a beautiful expression of that bond. Together, you can build a legacy of faith, love, and shared responsibility—laying a strong foundation for a future marked by abundance and joy.

Maintaining Intimacy Amidst Life's Demands

The demands of daily life—work, children, household chores, and the myriad responsibilities that fill our calendars—often leave little room for the tender intimacy that nourishes a marriage. We can become so engrossed in the practicalities of existence that the emotional and physical connections that bind us as husband and wife begin to fray. Yet, maintaining intimacy, both physical and emotional, is not merely a luxury; it's a vital necessity for a thriving, God-centered marriage. It's a reflection of the deep and abiding love that mirrors God's own love for us.

Prioritizing intimacy amidst the relentless pressures of life requires a conscious effort, a deliberate choice to set aside time and energy for connection. This isn't about scheduling romantic dates with the precision of a military operation, although those can certainly be beneficial. Rather, it's about creating a mindset where nurturing intimacy is a priority, woven into the fabric of daily life. It begins with recognizing the importance of small gestures, the seemingly insignificant moments that accumulate to form a powerful tapestry of love and affection. A gentle touch, a lingering hug, a shared smile across the kitchen table – these are the building blocks of enduring intimacy.

Communication is the lifeblood of any strong relationship, but especially vital when it comes to intimacy. Open and honest communication about needs, desires, and concerns is crucial. This isn't a one-time conversation; it's an ongoing dialogue, requiring both vulnerability and empathy. If one partner feels neglected or unloved, it's imperative to express those feelings without blame or accusation. Create a safe space where each partner feels comfortable sharing their needs, fears, and hopes. Active listening, truly hearing and understanding your spouse's perspective, is paramount.

Unspoken expectations can really throw a wrench in any relationship, often creating unnecessary distance and misunderstandings. Imagine one partner believing that intimacy shines through grand, sweeping gestures, like surprise getaways or extravagant gifts, while the other finds true closeness in the small, quiet moments—a warm cup of coffee shared on the couch or a lingering gaze during a sunset.

This difference in perception can easily lead to feelings of resentment and disconnection. That's why it's crucial to open up about what intimacy truly means to each other. Regular conversations about intimacy—its definition, its significance, and the ways it can be nurtured—can pave the path to a deeper bond. Remember, intimacy isn't just about physical closeness; it's a rich tapestry woven from emotional, spiritual, and intellectual connections. So, take the time to explore this beautiful complexity together.

We often find ourselves exhausted at the end of a long day, leaving little energy for romance. But physical intimacy is crucial for maintaining a deep connection. However, it's not just about the act itself; it's about the intentionality and affection that surround it. Making time for physical affection, even when tired, shows a commitment to nurturing the relationship. Consider small, tender acts of physical affection throughout the day—a hand-hold while walking, a back rub after a stressful event. These small gestures can significantly impact intimacy levels. If tiredness is a consistent barrier, exploring alternative times or approaches to physical intimacy could be beneficial.

But what happens when fatigue or stress become insurmountable obstacles? Sometimes, life's demands overshadow our desire for intimacy. Illness, job pressures, or family emergencies can temporarily disrupt the flow of intimacy. In such times, it's essential to practice grace and understanding. Acknowledge the external pressures, and focus on the small acts of connection that remain possible. A simple "I love you" or a comforting presence can speak volumes, even when physical intimacy feels unattainable. Remember that your love and commitment are not conditional upon outward expressions of intimacy.

Spiritual intimacy often serves as a strong foundation for physical and emotional intimacy. Shared faith, prayer, and worship can foster a deep sense of connection and unity. Praying together, reading scriptures aloud, or attending church services together strengthens the spiritual bond and creates a deeper understanding of each other's beliefs and values. This shared spiritual journey not only reinforces a couple's faith but also fosters a sense of shared purpose and meaning, strengthening your intimacy. When our lives are grounded in faith, we find strength, resilience, and a sense of peace that allows us to better navigate the challenges that life throws our way. It's through this shared spiritual journey that we can truly understand the depth of our love and our commitment to one another.

The pressures of daily life can indeed affect our intimacy, but prayer helps us to weather the storms. Taking time to pray together, both individually and as a couple, creates a powerful spiritual bond.

Sharing our struggles, anxieties, and hopes in prayer fosters empathy and understanding. It can help to alleviate stress and to find the strength to face challenges together. Prayer is a powerful tool for finding peace and healing within our marriage. Through prayer, we can align our relationship with God's will and find the grace to navigate the difficulties that stand in our way.

Finding time for connection in a busy world requires conscious effort and planning. It may involve creative scheduling, such as making time for a short walk together after dinner or having a conversation during the morning coffee. Regular date nights, even if just for an hour, can be vital for maintaining intimacy. Remember that even the smallest acts of connection can have a profound impact.

Regularly setting aside time for shared activities, such as a favorite hobby or a mutual interest, creates lasting memories and reaffirms your commitment to one another. Consider keeping a journal where you write down your appreciation for your partner, a reminder of their positive attributes, and how much they mean to you.

Nurturing intimacy is a continuous process, a lifelong journey that requires consistent effort, understanding, and prayer. It's about creating space for connection amidst the demands of daily life, recognizing the importance of both grand gestures and small moments of affection. It is a journey that is enriched by spiritual intimacy, strengthened by shared faith, and sustained by open and honest communication. Through consistent effort, faith, and love, you can build a marriage characterized by deep and lasting intimacy. Remember, this isn't about perfection, but rather about unwavering commitment to nurturing your bond, one prayer, one touch, one loving conversation at a time. The beauty of a God-centered marriage lies in this ongoing process of deepening connection, a journey shared with faith as your guide and love as your compass.

Finally, remember that intimacy is a dynamic process, ever-evolving throughout the various stages of marriage. As circumstances change—the arrival of children, career transitions, or aging parents—adjustments in how you nurture intimacy may be needed.

The key is to remain flexible, understanding, and committed to the ongoing process of connecting with each other on every level: physical, emotional, and spiritual. Through prayer, communication, and intentional effort, you can create a deeply intimate marriage that reflects the enduring love of God. Your marriage is a sacred covenant, a partnership blessed by God, and nurturing intimacy is a tangible expression of that sacred bond. Remember that God's love is a model for your own; His unfailing and unconditional love serves as an inspiration for your dedication to cultivating a loving and intimate relationship with your spouse.

Raising Godly Children

Imagine the vibrant tapestry of a God-centered marriage, intricately woven with threads of love, faith, and unwavering commitment.

This beautiful creation is not just a dance for the couple; it extends its embrace to their children—the cherished inheritors of their faith and values. Raising godly children in a nurturing, faith-filled home is more than an obligation; it's a divine calling—a golden opportunity to shape young hearts and minds for a life steeped in purpose and service to God. This incredible journey demands patience, understanding, and a steadfast dedication to modeling the principles we wish to pass on.

At the heart of this endeavor lies a strong, loving marriage. Children are like little sponges, keenly absorbing not just our words but our actions. Our marriage stands as a living testament to the power of God's love, showcasing the beauty of commitment, forgiveness, and mutual respect. When children see their parents support one another, they develop a secure sense of belonging and a blueprint for healthy relationships in their own lives. Yes, disagreements will happen; they are an inevitable part of any partnership. Yet, how we navigate those conflicts matters. By resolving issues with grace and humility, we teach our children that disagreements don't have to spiral into chaos but can be stepping stones for growth and deeper understanding.

Instilling faith in our children is a delightful journey that begins even before they can fully articulate their beliefs. From the moment they arrive in our world, we can weave faith into the fabric of their daily lives—praying before meals, sharing Bible stories, and singing joyful hymns. These seemingly small rituals create a comforting rhythm of faith. As our children grow, engaging them in age-appropriate discussions about their beliefs, and answering their questions honestly, nurtures a profound understanding of God's love in their lives. Family church outings, faith-based activities, and community service projects are also integral to solidifying their spiritual foundation. It's about creating a home where faith is not just talked about but fully lived—a vibrant connection with God that feels genuine and inviting.

Beyond the formalities of faith, instilling strong moral values is essential. This isn't just a checklist of rules; it's about cultivating character. We can achieve this by modeling integrity, honesty, compassion, and kindness in our daily lives. Our children learn best through our actions, not just our words. When they see us committed to ethical conduct—even in challenging situations— they absorb valuable lessons without us needing to spell them out. Consistent, loving discipline is equally important. It's not about punishment; it's about guidance and correction, equipping our children to make responsible choices. We're shaping their character to reflect the attributes of Christ—instilling patience, forgiveness, and self-control.

Creating a warm and nurturing home is at the heart of parenting, where every child deserves to feel cherished, valued, and understood. Picture a safe haven filled with laughter and comfort, where clear expectations and consistent routines provide a sense of security. Open communication plays a vital role, allowing children to share their feelings without fear of judgment. When we listen attentively and validate their emotions, we build a foundation of trust and intimacy. These connections create a haven that encourages growth and emotional well-being.

Of course, parenting comes with its own set of challenges. The trials of adolescence, peer pressure, and behavioral hurdles require not just patience but also an abundance of love and wisdom. In a world inundated with secular messages, our faith can be that steady anchor we all need. Prayer becomes an essential lifeline, helping us tap into divine wisdom and grace. Don't hesitate to reach out to trusted mentors, pastors, or counselors for guidance; their insight can be invaluable during tough times.

Integrating faith into our parenting isn't just about rules; it's about creating shared experiences that reinforce our values. Think of family movie nights with uplifting films, reading books that inspire, or engaging in community service together. Whether it's volunteering at a local charity or simply gathering for family prayer, these moments strengthen our bonds and instill a sense of belonging. Regular family devotions—where scripture comes alive and discussions flow—solidify our commitment to faith as a family.

When it comes to discipline, remember: it's less about punishment and more about guidance. Approach each lesson with love and understanding. Help children grasp the consequences of their choices and encourage them to take responsibility, fostering growth rather than fear. Consistency is key; children thrive when the rules are clear and fairly enforced. Instead of focusing on control, aim to empower them to make positive choices.

Encouraging kids to actively engage with their faith is crucial. Foster their personal relationship with God through prayer, Bible study, and worship experiences. Encourage participation in youth groups or mission trips, allowing them to connect with peers who share their journey. Providing opportunities for service not only instills empathy and compassion but also helps them discover their purpose in extending love to others.

Remember, the journey of parenting is a marathon, not a sprint. There will be joyful moments alongside inevitable challenges. Throughout this journey, let your faith shine as your guiding light, offering strength and wisdom. It's about creating a legacy of faith— one that shapes a generation filled with love for God and a commitment to serve others.

Ultimately, our role as parents isn't to create perfect children but to guide them toward a genuine relationship with God. We are their mentors, advocates, and role models. As we instill faith, values, and morals, we trust that God will work within their hearts, guiding them on their unique paths. Our prayers for them will become a rhythm of trust in God's grace as they grow in purpose, meaning, and unwavering faith.

Raising godly children is both a profound privilege and a responsible commitment we embrace with humility and prayer. This journey reflects our love for God and is a testament to our dedication. As we share our love, instill values, and demonstrate faith, we lay the groundwork for a legacy that will resonate far beyond our lifetimes. Our hope is to see our children grow into strong, compassionate, and faith-filled individuals, serving as reflections of Christ in all their endeavors. This journey, filled with challenges and blessings, is ultimately about love, grace, and the enriching rewards from God, making every step worthwhile.

CHAPTER 3

THE POWER OF SHARED PURPOSE

The journey of faith isn't just a solitary path; it's a vibrant tapestry woven from the threads of shared experiences, mutual support, and a unified purpose. As a couple deeply committed to Christ, we've found that our most fulfilling moments arise from a shared mission—a collaborative effort to serve God and positively impact the world around us. But this shared mission doesn't simply materialize overnight; it's a beautiful process of introspection, heartfelt communication, and prayerful discernment.

To start uncovering your shared mission, dive into your own individual soul-searching. Carve out time for quiet reflection, seeking God's guidance through prayer and meditation. Ask yourselves some powerful questions: What ignites your passions? What unique gifts has God given each of you? Which causes truly resonate with your hearts? These questions are more than mere exercises; they're essential steps toward understanding God's unique blueprint for your lives. Perhaps one of you has a natural gift for teaching, while the other thrives in community service. Or maybe one is drawn to artistic expression, while the other excels in logical problem-solving.

Instead of viewing these differences as divides, embrace them as complementary strengths that can combine to create an unstoppable force for good.

But remember, this introspection shouldn't happen in isolation. Open, honest communication is key. Share your discoveries with each other, listening intently to your spouse's reflections. Create a safe haven where vulnerability is embraced and honesty is cherished. This shared vulnerability will lead to deeper understanding and, ultimately, a clearer shared vision. Talk about your hopes, dreams, and fears, acknowledging that living a God-centered life doesn't come without its challenges. It's within those struggles that your faith will be tested and refined, drawing you closer together.

As you progress through your individual reflections and honest conversations, begin to identify your shared values and passions. What core principles guide your lives? Are you both passionate about social justice, environmental stewardship, or perhaps nurturing spiritual growth within your community? Pinpointing these shared values will act as the cornerstone of your mission together. If you both have a deep conviction to help those in need, why not volunteer at a local homeless shelter? If you share a love for children, consider mentoring underprivileged youth or sponsoring a child in need. The possibilities are endless once you discover the common ground that fuels your shared commitment.

It's essential to remember that your shared mission is like a living, breathing entity—constantly evolving and changing as you walk through life together. Think of it as a beautiful journey filled with twists and turns, often leading you to unexpected places and opportunities. Embrace the idea that new paths may unfold right before you, guiding you to ways of serving others you might never have imagined. Staying open to change and communicating with each other is key to keeping your mission vibrant and relevant throughout your lives.

As you embark on this mission together, take a moment to identify your unique strengths. This isn't about competing or showing off; it's about celebrating the special gifts God has bestowed upon you as a couple. Maybe one of you has a knack for organizing, while the other is a brilliant communicator. Or perhaps one is a natural problem-solver, while the other brings a compassionate ear. By recognizing these individual talents, you can harness your combined abilities, making your efforts more effective. Imagine how powerful it would be if one spouse is a fundraising whiz and the other a gifted speaker—together, you could create a dynamic force for a charitable cause!

Integrating your faith into this shared mission is another vital element. Your purpose should be deeply rooted in your beliefs, reflecting your dedication to serving God and His people. This isn't about preaching or imposing your views; it's about living out your faith authentically through your actions. Whether it's leading a Bible study group, volunteering at your local church, or simply making prayer a daily ritual, ensure that your faith is woven seamlessly into the fabric of your mission. It's about becoming a living embodiment of Christ's love, radiating compassion and kindness wherever you go.

Let's dive into some inspiring examples! Picture a couple passionate about environmental stewardship. They might host community clean-up events, rallying their neighbors to view nature as a sacred gift from God. Or consider a couple devoted to education; they could volunteer as tutors in underprivileged schools, not just to teach academics but to instill values and guidance that uplift future generations.

Now think about a couple who feels called to help the homeless. They could establish a community outreach program, offering food and shelter to those in need. Their faith would illuminate the reality that each person they serve is a cherished child of God, worthy of respect and compassion. Their mission goes beyond just providing meals; it's about restoring dignity and hope to those who often feel invisible.

And remember, your mission isn't solely about grand gestures or big events. Often, it's the little things—a warm smile, a kind word, a listening ear—that resonate the most with others. These small acts of love and service, done with genuine faith and a spirit of kindness, can create ripples of change in ways you might not even recognize. They enrich your lives and create a profound impact in your community, deepening your connection to each other and to God.

So, as you continue on this journey, stay flexible, embrace your strengths, let your faith guide you, and never underestimate the power of small acts of love. Your shared mission has the potential to bless not just those around you but also each other in incredible ways.

Embarking on the journey of defining and achieving your shared mission is an adventure like no other—one filled with twists and turns that test your resolve and deepen your connection. As you navigate this path, you'll inevitably face challenges, setbacks, and moments of uncertainty. But guess what? These hurdles are not just obstacles; they are opportunities for growth! They'll challenge your faith and strengthen your relationship, pushing you to discover just how resilient you can be together.

In these moments, lean on each other. Embrace prayer and mutual support as your guiding lights. By staying committed to your shared purpose, you'll not only push through the tough times but also emerge stronger and more united in your mission. Imagine standing together, hand in hand, having conquered the trials that once seemed daunting!

Don't forget to pause along the way to celebrate your victories—no matter how small they may seem. Each step forward is worth acknowledging! These celebrations reignite your spirit and bolster your determination, reminding you of the incredible impact you are making together. Your journey of faith is a rich tapestry of learning, growth, and service; it's here that you'll uncover the true power of your shared purpose.

Remember, your shared mission isn't just about reaching a destination; it's about forging deeper intimacy with God, with one another, and with the world around you. So, embrace this journey fully. Let your shared faith light the way toward a life brimming with purpose and meaning. The blessings you cultivate will be limitless, and the echoes of your impact will resonate long after you're gone. Together, you have the potential to change lives— starting with your own!

Serving Others Together

Serving others together isn't merely an act of charity; it's a powerful catalyst for marital unity and spiritual growth. The Bible repeatedly emphasizes the importance of love, compassion, and generosity, urging us to be "good stewards" of the gifts God has bestowed upon us. When we channel these gifts into service to others, as a couple, we experience a profound deepening of our bond, a strengthening of our faith, and a tangible manifestation of God's love in the world.

Think of the parable of the Good Samaritan. The Samaritan, a member of a despised group, shows extraordinary compassion to a stranger in need. This act of selfless service transcends societal boundaries and embodies the very essence of Christ's teachings. As a couple, we can strive to emulate the Samaritan's compassion, extending our hands to those who are suffering, marginalized, or forgotten.

This service might take many forms. Consider the couple who dedicates their weekends to volunteering at a local soup kitchen. The shared experience of preparing and serving meals, the shared conversation with those they serve, creates a unique bonding experience. It's not just about the physical act of serving food; it's about the connection forged through shared empathy, shared purpose, and a shared commitment to serving Christ.

Or imagine a couple who tutors children in underprivileged neighborhoods. The patience, the dedication, the joy of witnessing a child's understanding blossom – these are shared experiences that enrich their marriage and deepen their spiritual connection. Their shared act of service allows them to impart not only academic knowledge but also moral values and a sense of hope. It's a tangible way of investing in the future, building a better world, one child at a time.

Another example could be a couple who chooses to mentor young adults navigating challenging life transitions. The wisdom shared, the guidance offered, the empathy shown— these are acts of service that ripple outwards, impacting multiple lives. It's a privilege to guide another along their path, and doing so together fosters intimacy and a shared sense of purpose.

Serving together doesn't necessitate grand gestures; it often resides in the small, everyday acts of kindness and compassion. A simple phone call to a lonely neighbor, offering a helping hand to an elderly relative, visiting someone in the hospital – these seemingly insignificant acts, performed consistently with love and faith, speak volumes about the depth of your commitment to one another and to God.

Consider the impact of regularly visiting nursing homes. The companionship offered, the stories shared, the simple act of holding a hand – these are profoundly significant acts of service, strengthening both your bond and your faith. It's an opportunity to learn, to listen, and to connect with a generation that often feels overlooked.

You might consider fostering or adopting a child in need. This profound act of service not only transforms the life of a child, but it irrevocably alters the lives of the couple, deepening their love and compassion in ways that only this kind of shared commitment can achieve. The shared joys, challenges, and rewards of raising a child, especially one who needs extra love and support, strengthens a couple's bond in profound ways, enriching their spiritual walk.

Even seemingly mundane tasks can be infused with a profound spiritual dimension when approached with a heart of service. Consider preparing a meal for a family in need or providing childcare for a stressed-out friend. These acts, born of love and compassion, are powerful expressions of faith in action.

It's vital to remember that serving others together is not merely about the actions themselves; it's about the shared intention and the spirit behind the actions. Prayer is an integral part of this process. Praying together before, during, and after your acts of service is a powerful way to invite God's guidance and blessing into your shared endeavors. It allows you to approach your service with humility, acknowledging that you are instruments of God's love and grace.

Further enriching the experience is reflecting together after each act of service. Discuss what you experienced, what you learned, and how God worked through you. Sharing these reflections strengthens your bond and deepens your understanding of God's purpose in your lives.

Remember that challenges and setbacks will inevitably arise. Times of discouragement are opportunities for prayer and mutual support. The struggles encountered in your service will strengthen your faith and refine your commitment to one another. Remember, it's not about perfection; it's about perseverance, fueled by unwavering faith and mutual love.

The journey of serving others together is not a destination, but a continuous process of learning, growth, and mutual support. Embrace this journey with open hearts and unwavering faith, for in serving others, you are truly serving God, strengthening your marriage, and enriching your spiritual lives. The rewards are immeasurable, the impact profound, and the blessings abundant. The journey of shared service, rooted in a shared faith, is a path that leads to a deeper, more fulfilling relationship with God, with each other, and with the world around you.

Building a Legacy of Faith

Building a legacy isn't about erecting monuments or amassing wealth; it's about shaping hearts and minds, leaving an imprint of faith on the sands of time. As a couple, deeply rooted in our faith, we believe that our most significant legacy will be the spiritual inheritance we pass down to our children and grandchildren – a legacy woven not just with words, but with the very fabric of our lives. It's a legacy built not in grand gestures, but in the quiet, everyday moments that speak volumes about our values, beliefs, and unwavering devotion to God.

Like many things, our journey in building this legacy began with prayer. We knell together, seeking God's guidance, asking for wisdom, and humbly acknowledging that our ability to raise children in the faith is a gift, a responsibility bestowed upon us. We understand that we aren't simply raising children; we are cultivating disciples, planting seeds of faith that we prayed would blossom into mature, vibrant expressions of God's love.

One of the most profound ways we can seek to instill faith in our children is through consistent, intentional family devotions. These aren't just perfunctory rituals; they are sacred spaces where we connect with God and with each other. We read scripture together, sometimes taking turns reading aloud, sometimes engaging in lively discussions about the passages we read. We pray together, voicing our concerns, expressing our gratitude, and interceding for others. These moments of shared faith become sacred threads that weave together the tapestry of our family life. It isn't about lengthy, formal prayers but genuine connection, vulnerability, and honest conversation about our faith.

We need to incorporate age-appropriate Bible stories, letting the narratives inspire wonder, empathy and curiosity. Discussions would often wander into life lessons and relevant contemporary situations, helping them to understand the application of biblical principles to daily living.

Beyond formal devotions, we need to infuse our faith into the everyday fabric of our family life. Pray before meals, expressing gratitude for the simple blessings we enjoy. Engage in charitable acts together, volunteering at local shelters, assisting elderly neighbors, and participating in community service projects. These aren't just acts of service; they are lessons in compassion, empathy, and loving our neighbor. It isn't always easy. There are times of resistance, challenging questions, and moments of doubt, but through consistent engagement, open communication, and always making faith the priority, the benefits will far surpass the challenges. These moments, small as they may seem, become powerful, lasting memories which instill deep values.

We also nee to intentionally integrate faith into our celebrations and traditions. Christmas isn't just about presents; it is about the celebration of the birth of Jesus Christ. Easter isn't about Easter eggs; it was about the resurrection and the hope of eternal life. Attended church services regularly, not as a chore, but as an integral part of family life. Seek out a church community that share your values and support your efforts to raise your children in faith. This community becomes an extension of your family, a supportive network where your children can grow spiritually and socially, surrounded by like-minded individuals. Also ensure that your children participate in church youth groups, Sunday school, and church camps. This fosters a sense of belonging and community, enriching their spiritual lives beyond the confines of your home.

Another essential aspect of building a legacy of faith is leading by example. Our children learn more from observing our actions than from hearing our words. They witness our unwavering commitment to our faith, our dedication to prayer, our love for one another, and our commitment to serving others. We should strive to create a home environment filled with love, respect, and forgiveness; and make sure they understand the value of integrity, honesty, and compassion. We need to acknowledge that we are not perfect, and mistakes will happen. However, the important thing is to model repentance, forgiveness, and reconciliation. These experiences help them learn to navigate the complexities of life with grace and humility, grounding them in their faith.

In our conversations, we should actively engage with their questions about faith, allowing for doubts and struggles to be openly discussed. Don't shy away from difficult theological concepts, adapt our explanations to their age and understanding. We should encourage them to read the Bible for themselves, to develop their own relationship with God, to explore their own faith journey, emphasizing the importance of developing a personal relationship with Jesus. It isn't about forcing them to believe, but about guiding them towards a faith that was their own, rooted in understanding and experience.

It is also essential to understand the importance of mentorship. Actively seek godly mentors who can guide and support your parenting journey. These mentors will share their wisdom and experiences, offering invaluable insights and helping us navigate the challenges of raising our children in a world that often seems hostile to faith. The wisdom from experienced mentors helps avoid pitfalls and gives us the tools and perspective to handle challenging situations.

Beyond your immediate family, you should seek ways to extend your legacy of faith to the broader community. Support faith-based organizations, volunteer time and resources to those in need, and engage in acts of service that reflect your commitment to God's love. This not only instills in our children a deep sense of social responsibility but also deepens our own faith. Being active participants in the community demonstrates the value of a life lived in service to others, extending the reach of our faith beyond the confines of our home.

It's a continual process, this building of a legacy. There will be challenges, moments of doubt, and times when we may feel we've fallen short. But the key is not perfection, but perseverance. A consistent commitment, fueled by prayer and guided by a strong conviction of our faith, sustains our efforts. The goal is to create a spiritual heritage rich in faith, love, and service, not just for our children, but for generations to come. The hope is that the legacy will continue to ripple outwards, touching lives and inspiring others to live a life that glorifies God. This is the legacy we aim to leave - one that not only endures but also inspires others to build their own lasting faith-based legacies. It's a journey of faith, a shared commitment, and a testament to the enduring power of a life lived for God.

Celebrating Milestones and Blessings

Celebrating the milestones in life is so much more than just marking the passage of time; it's a beautiful opportunity to acknowledge God's faithfulness and rejoice in His abundant grace. As a couple, making the effort to celebrate both the significant moments and the little victories can profoundly strengthen your bond and deepen your gratitude for one another. Think of it as a conscious choice to pause amidst the hustle and bustle of everyday life to truly recognize and appreciate the blessings that God has poured into your lives.

These celebrations don't have to be extravagant; in fact, it's often the simplest moments that become the most sacred. Picture yourselves creating spaces—perhaps a cozy dinner at home or a peaceful walk in nature—where you can express your gratitude for each other and for God's unwavering love. It's an invitation to savor the sweetness of your journey together.

One of the most powerful ways to make these milestones meaningful is through heartfelt expressions of gratitude. Take a moment to reflect on what you truly appreciate about one another. It's not enough to feel thankful; saying it out loud adds depth to your connection. Make it a habit to share phrases like, "I appreciate you," or "Thank you for…" followed by something specific that speaks to the essence of your partner. This practice becomes a beautiful language of love, serving as a constant reminder of your commitment and admiration for each other.

Don't stop at words! Bring your appreciation to life with small, tangible gestures. A handwritten note tucked into a briefcase, a thoughtful little gift that recalls a cherished moment, or even a simple act of service—these acts of love don't require grand designs; what matters most is the thought and intention behind them. A favorite book or a cozy night spent in prayer can speak volumes about your devotion. These small, meaningful gestures reinforce the beauty of your connection and your commitment to one another.

And don't underestimate the power of reflection. At the end of each year, set aside some time to look back on the past twelve months—not just to celebrate achievements but to learn from challenges and count the blessings you've received. Reflect on how God has guided you through ups and downs, how He has protected you, and how He has provided for your needs. Consider writing your thoughts in a journal—it's a powerful way to explore your journey together and recognize how your faith has evolved.

When it comes to anniversaries, don't see them merely as dates on a calendar. Make them moments of renewal, reaffirming your commitment to each other and to God. Celebrate with intention: perhaps a quiet evening filled with prayer, a special meal cooked together, or even a weekend getaway to reignite that spark and strengthen your connection. These occasions become cherished opportunities to acknowledge the vows you've made and to celebrate the beautiful journey you've traveled together.

By creating and honoring these moments, you're not just celebrating milestones; you're weaving gratitude and love into the very fabric of your relationship. Let each celebration deepen your bond and draw you closer to each other and to God!

Celebrations hold special significance in our lives, and they become even more meaningful when we weave acts of service into the fabric of our festivities. Imagine this: instead of just celebrating a birthday with parties and presents, you choose to spend time volunteering at a local soup kitchen. What about commemorating an anniversary by contributing to a charity that resonates with your heart? These actions speak volumes about your commitment to gratitude and faith, transforming a simple celebration into a powerful expression of love, compassion, and generosity. There's an incredible joy in sharing your blessings, and this selfless spirit not only uplifts those around you but also enriches your own spiritual journey.

At the core of celebrating milestones is a heartfelt attitude of gratitude. This isn't just a fleeting feeling; it's a conscious choice to shine a light on the good in our lives, to cherish those everyday miracles, and to recognize the divine hand guiding us through it all. When you embrace gratitude, you're embarking on a spiritual discipline that alters your outlook, deepening your relationship with God and with each other. It's about savoring joy and finding contentment by focusing on blessings instead of shortcomings.

Let's not forget that celebrating milestones is as much about the journey as it is about the destination. Life is a beautiful tapestry woven with ups and downs, trials and triumphs. Acknowledging this journey—in all its messy, glorious wonder—is just as essential as celebrating achievements. It means embracing the struggles that have shaped you, the lessons learned along the way, and the strength gained together. This process of reflection and celebration fortifies your trust in each other and nurtures faith in God's provision.

And while the big milestones matter, it's the small victories and daily blessings that often bring the most joy. Take a moment to appreciate life's simple pleasures: the warmth of a sunset, the laughter of your children, or an unexpectedly delightful meal with loved ones. Each small moment recognized becomes a beacon of light, guiding you along your journey of faith and gratitude.

Crucially, remember that celebrating milestones isn't about self-aggrandizement; it's a chance to acknowledge God's grace and express heartfelt appreciation for His blessings. It's about sharing joy, uplifting one another, and inspiring those around you to lead lives filled with purpose and faith. Together, you can nurture a culture of gratitude—within your marriage and beyond.

Consider creating unique traditions that enhance your milestone celebrations. Ever thought about starting a "Gratitude Jar?" Write down the little things you're thankful for throughout the year. Then, on special occasions, gather to read through those entries. This simple act becomes a profound reminder of God's faithfulness and the abundant blessings we sometimes overlook.

Don't forget to capture your journey with photo albums and scrapbooks! These visual stories of your shared experiences serve as constant reminders of God's hand in your lives, reinforcing your bond and commitment to one another. They celebrate the milestones and everyday moments that together shape the narrative of your love and faith.

Finally, keep in mind that honoring milestones is an ongoing journey, not just a one-time event. It's about continually recognizing God's grace, expressing appreciation for His gifts, and spreading joy to those around you. This journey of faith showcases the enduring power of love and highlights God's presence in your lives. By intentionally celebrating both the grand and the humble moments, you strengthen your connection as a couple, deepen your relationship with God, and leave a legacy of gratitude and faith for generations to come. Embrace this consistent practice of gratitude, and watch as it transforms your life into a tapestry of celebration and hope for all to witness.

Navigating Seasons of Change

Life can be an unpredictable ride, full of unexpected twists and turns. You often find that navigating the highs and lows isn't a solo journey but one best undertaken hand in hand, with God as your unwavering guide. The bond of shared faith becomes your anchor, keeping you steady amid the storms that life throws your way. Rather than viewing transitions as hurdles, you'll start to see them as golden opportunities for growth—moments that deepen your connection and strengthen your reliance on God's unchanging love.

One poignant example many couples encounter is a career transition. Picture this: a husband, once settled and satisfied in his job, suddenly feels a powerful nudge toward a new path—a calling that resonates deeply with what he believes is God's purpose for his life. This decision is anything but simple. It involves stepping away from the comfort of the familiar and plunging into the uncertainty of the unknown. It's natural for fear, doubt, and a hint of resentment to creep in. The financial stakes can feel overwhelming, and the fear of failure looms large.

Yet, instead of succumbing to anxiety, they choose a different approach—one rooted in prayer and mutual support. Countless hours are spent in heartfelt conversation and prayer, seeking clarity and reassurance from God. They openly share their fears and concerns, ensuring each voice is heard and understood. This process of discerning God's will transforms into a shared adventure, weaving their lives together even more tightly and solidifying their faith.

During this transformative period, their shared faith becomes a lifeline. They lean on each other for emotional support, offering uplifting words during moments of doubt. Together, they commit to nurturing a vibrant prayer life, both individually and as a couple. They find refuge in scripture, drawing wisdom and strength from verses that remind them of God's faithfulness and provision. Constant reminders echo between them: God's plans for their lives far exceed their imagination, and His love remains a constant source of comfort, even when the road ahead feels uncertain.

Navigating life's changes can feel overwhelming, but embracing practical strategies can truly make a difference. One couple discovered this firsthand as they faced financial uncertainties. They rolled up their sleeves and crafted a realistic budget, fully aware of the income fluctuations that lay ahead. Seeking guidance from trusted mentors and advisors, they gained invaluable insights, reminding them that they weren't alone on this journey. With each small victory celebrated, they acknowledged that every step forward was a testament to God's faithfulness. Through this process, they cultivated a positive outlook, choosing to focus on the opportunities before them instead of the challenges looming behind.

But change doesn't just come in forms we expect—sometimes it arrives as health challenges. Whether it's a physical setback or emotional turmoil, these times can truly test the bonds of any relationship. During such seasons, the power of empathy, patience, and unwavering support becomes paramount. Open communication is essential; sharing your fears and concerns in honest, vulnerable conversations can strengthen your connection. Here, faith plays an extraordinary role, offering strength and solace. Many find comfort in scripture passages that highlight God's presence during times of suffering, and prayer transforms into a lifeline, providing strength, peace, and perseverance when it's needed most.

Maintaining a sense of normalcy is crucial, even when life seems turned upside down. Continue with your rituals: prayer, Bible study, shared moments together. These routines offer a stabilizing force, grounding you amidst the upheaval. Your church community and trusted friends can become a remarkable support network, providing encouragement, practical help, and a sense of belonging when you need it the most.

Family transitions can be remarkable, transformative events that shape the very fabric of your marital bond. Whether it's the exhilarating joy of welcoming a new child, the poignant moment when they leave for college or start their careers, or the demanding task of caring for aging parents, each phase brings its own unique set of challenges. Navigating these transitions with grace and a sense of purpose requires dedication to maintaining open communication, mutual respect, and a shared understanding of one another's responsibilities.

When children enter the picture, the responsibility of raising them in a nurturing, faith-centered environment comes to the forefront. This calls for intentionality—think family prayers, Bible study sessions, and regular church attendance. Creating a home that fosters spiritual growth takes effort and time management, but the rewards are immeasurable. Imagine those moments when your family gathers to share their thoughts on faith, helping to cultivate a lasting sense of togetherness.

As your kids venture into adolescence and young adulthood, you find yourself facing a new set of challenges. This unpredictable stage demands patience, understanding, and unwavering support. You start to realize that sometimes, the best way to guide them is by listening more than speaking. This period becomes a dance of mutual respect, where your shared faith acts as a beacon during turbulent times, reminding you both of God's unbreakable love and guidance.

Then comes the bittersweet moment when your children leave home to begin their own adventures. It's a time filled with both pride and nostalgia, requiring you to redefine your roles as a couple. Embracing this change isn't always easy, but leaning into your faith and supporting one another helps bridge the gap. Your rooted spiritual foundation serves as a steady anchor, allowing you to celebrate your children's growth while also nurturing your relationship.

Caring for aging parents introduces its own complexities—a mix of joy and challenge that reshapes your day-to-day lives. This experience tests your patience and adaptability, but it also provides a platform for expressing love and gratitude. Engaging your children in caring for their grandparents not only strengthens family bonds but also builds lasting memories that will resonate through generations. With faith guiding you, you'll find strength and peace, trusting in God's grace during these testing times.

In every season of change, your shared faith offers direction, illuminating the path through uncertainty and deepening your bond as a couple. You'll discover that embracing life's transitions requires more than just faith; it takes open dialogue, a willingness to grow together, and unwavering support for one another.

Ultimately, these experiences will enrich your relationship with God and each other, fortifying your resilience and trust in His divine plan. With faith as your cornerstone, you'll navigate life's transitions hand in hand, filled with hope, love, and an unwavering faith in God's grace. Embrace these moments together, as they are not just challenges but opportunities for growth, connection, and renewed strength.

CHAPTER 4

SPIRITUAL DISCIPLINES FOR COUPLES

The foundation of our shared faith is not just about passively accepting beliefs; it's about embarking on an exciting journey of connection with God. One of the most enriching aspects of nurturing this vibrant relationship, especially as a couple, is the practice of consistent Bible study. Think of it as more than just reading; it's diving into an adventure together—immersing yourselves in the stories, grappling with their meanings, and allowing the scriptures to shape your hearts and actions in unity.

Imagine the Bible as a beautifully penned love letter from God, crafted over thousands of years, revealing His heart, character, and His grand plan for humanity. When you approach it side-by-side, you unlock a treasure trove of insight, deepening your understanding of each other while strengthening your bond as partners in faith. Picture yourself exploring passages that resonate with your life right now—discussing what they mean for your marriage, your work, your parenting, and even your personal hurdles. This isn't just an intellectual exercise; it's about experiencing God's transformative power together, weaving His truths into the very fabric of your relationship.

Yet, many couples grapple with fitting Bible study into their bustling lives. With work, family, and social commitments tugging at your time, spiritual disciplines might slip down the priority list. But here's the good news: prioritizing this practice can lead to immeasurable rewards! It's about cultivating a habit that works for you, even if it's just for fifteen minutes a day. Find those moments that fit your routine—maybe it's a peaceful morning before the day kicks off, a quiet lunch break, or snuggling up in the evening. The magic is in making it consistent.

There are so many creative ways to explore scripture together! One enjoyable approach is to pick a specific book of the Bible and read through it together—perhaps a chapter a day or a couple of chapters each week. This structured method allows you to dig deeply into the stories and themes. For instance, you could unravel the wisdom of Proverbs, reflecting on the practical guidance it offers for your daily life, or journey through the Gospel of John, contemplating the life and teachings of Jesus Christ and how His example impacts your relationship with each other and with God.

Dive into the enriching experience of thematic Bible study! Imagine choosing a captivating theme—like forgiveness, love, or faith—and embarking on a journey through scripture together. This flexible approach allows you to connect deeply with the Bible in a way that truly speaks to your current experiences. Picture this: if you're navigating a challenging moment in your marriage, you might explore passages on forgiveness and reconciliation. As you uncover God's wisdom, you'll find guidance to help resolve your differences and strengthen your bond.

Another fantastic way to enhance your study is by using a devotional guide or commentary. These resources can illuminate biblical passages with practical insights, making your exploration easier and more rewarding. Couples' devotionals often come equipped with thoughtful questions for discussion, encouraging deep reflection and dialogue about your shared faith. Think of it as a supportive framework for your study, making it easier to dive into meaningful conversations right from the start.

Now, as you read together, challenge yourselves with engaging questions. Ask, "What's the heart of this passage? How does it connect to our lives?" Use these prompts as launch pads for sincere discussions. Talk about your thoughts and feelings openly, allowing these conversations to deepen your understanding of scripture and reinforce the connection between you. And remember, moments of silence can be powerful, too. Take time to bask in the presence of God's Word, letting it resonate within your hearts.

Don't shy away from disagreements; instead, embrace them as opportunities for growth! Respectful dialogue driven by a genuine desire to understand each other's perspectives can reveal new insights into the text and bring you closer together. Keep in mind that you're on a journey of discovery as a couple, and varying interpretations can enrich the experience. Approach your study with humility and a willingness to learn from each other.

Make it a point to weave what you learn into your daily lives. The Bible isn't just a historical text; it's alive and meant to transform every aspect of who we are. After exploring passages on love or compassion, brainstorm together on how you can actively practice these qualities in your relationship. If forgiveness is your focus, commit to exercising that principle daily. By consistently applying biblical teachings, you'll strengthen not only your faith but also your connection with each other.

Why not make Bible study a regular feature of your date nights? Instead of the usual dinner or a movie, carve out an evening dedicated to exploring God's Word together. This time creates a sacred space that fosters both intimacy and spiritual growth. Keep the atmosphere cozy: light some candles, play soft music, or enjoy a cup of tea while you discuss profound truths and personal revelations.

Add a creative twist to your study, too! You could journal your thoughts, draw or paint scenes that resonate with your readings, or even create a scrapbook that chronicles your scriptural journey together. Engage with the Word in a way that feels fresh and vibrant—perhaps even pen a song or a poem inspired by passages that touch your hearts. These creative outlets not only enhance your study but also deepen your faith.

Above all, remember that daily Bible study is not just about ticking a box on your spiritual checklist. It's about cultivating a genuine relationship with God and with each other, allowing His Word to transform your lives in profound ways. It's about finding guidance and strength during trying times and celebrating the blessings together. By anchoring your marriage in God's unwavering love and grace, you make the journey a shared adventure of faith. The rewards are immeasurable, far surpassing any effort you put in.

Embrace this sacred time, and watch your love for God and each other flourish in beautiful and unexpected ways. Through consistent Bible study, you will uncover the richness of God's Word, the depth of your love for one another, and the unwavering strength of your shared faith. Though there may be challenges along the way, the eternal rewards are worth every moment! So, dive in together and experience the transformative power of scripture in your lives.

The Practice of Regular Prayer

Building on the foundation of consistent Bible study, let's dive into another vital pillar of a vibrant spiritual life as a couple: regular prayer. Picture this: prayer isn't just a list of requests sent into the void; it's a lively, ongoing dialogue with the very heart of God. It's about creating communion that deepens your intimacy, both with Him and with each other. This beautiful practice infuses life into your relationship and shapes how you understand His purpose for your lives together.

Imagine standing shoulder to shoulder before the Creator of the universe. You share your joys, sorrows, hopes, and fears—each word a thread weaving your hearts closer together. This intimate exchange not only strengthens your bond with God but also cultivates a deeper connection between you two. Prayer is not a passive task; it's an energetic dance of love and grace, where you learn to listen to His gentle whispers and respond with open hearts.

Now, let's be real. Many couples look at the idea of "prayer time" and feel a wave of anxiety wash over them. They picture lengthy, formal sessions filled with eloquent words and an unrealistic standard of spiritual perfection. But here's the good news: true prayer is so much more accessible! It can be as simple as a whispered conversation over morning coffee, a quiet moment of reflection during a hectic day, or a heartfelt talk before bedtime. Remember, it's not about the length or the grandeur of your words, but about sincerity and a consistent connection.

Start small. Maybe set aside just five minutes each morning, holding hands and thanking God for the new day ahead. You can express gratitude for specific blessings—your family, your health, the roof over your heads, or even the strength to tackle challenges. This practice of shared gratitude will not only uplift your spirits but also set a positive tone for the day, reminding you that you're navigating life together, both as partners and as companions in faith.

As you grow more comfortable, feel free to extend that prayer time. Whether it's fifteen minutes, half an hour, or even an hour, what matters is the consistency. Make prayer a regular fixture in your daily routine—a sacred space where life slows down, and you can connect with God and each other on a deeper level. Reframe it from a chore to be checked off to a cherished rendezvous, a sacred time of intimate communion.

Don't hesitate to explore different ways to pray together! One engaging method is conversational prayer, where you simply chat with God like you would with a trusted friend. Share your thoughts, feelings, and experiences, both big and small. Forget formalities; let your words flow naturally. Speak freely, laying bare your hearts before God, and encourage one another to express your heartfelt vulnerabilities without fear of judgment. This mutual honesty creates a powerful bond, pulling you closer to each other and enveloping you both in His love.

Another enriching approach is intercessory prayer. This is where you pray for others—your family, friends, your church community, or anyone in need. Shift that focus outward and witness compassion blossom in your hearts. By lifting others in prayer, you cultivate empathy and reinforce your connection as you journey together, interceding for those around you.

Consider weaving contemplative prayer into your routine as well. This quiet practice allows you to settle the mind and focus on God's presence. Take a moment to simply be with Him, listening for His gentle voice. Perhaps meditate on a scripture or dwell in the melody of a hymn. Contemplative prayer can be profoundly healing, instilling peace and calm, both individually and as a couple. This shared stillness breeds a deep sense of intimacy and connection that transcends the chaos of everyday life.

As you nurture your shared prayer life, remember that listening actively is key. Prayer is a two-way conversation, not a monologue. Pay attention to God's guidance and direction. He often speaks to us through His Word, the experiences of our lives, and the gentle nudges of the Spirit. Learn to recognize His voice, trust His lead, and share these promptings with each other. Discussing your insights can clarify God's will for your marriage and your personal journeys.

Lastly, infuse prayer into every aspect of your lives. Don't limit it to specific times; let it flow freely throughout your daily experiences. Pray before meals, during important decisions, while facing stress, and in joyful moments alike. When challenges arise, let prayer be your first instinct. Make it a shared practice, bringing your concerns to God together and seeking His wisdom.

Remember, there may be times when prayer feels challenging. You might wrestle with doubts, encounter feelings of disconnection, or face spiritual dryness. That's completely normal! Prayer is a journey, not a destination. Even when your words feel empty, press on with unwavering faith. God knows our struggles intimately. Lean into Him, and watch how your relationship flourishes through both the highs and lows.

One powerful way to deepen your spiritual connection as a couple is to embark on the journey of a shared prayer journal. Imagine having a special place—whether it's a beautiful physical journal or a cozy digital document—where both of you can pour out your prayers, reflections, and experiences of God's presence in your lives. This isn't just journaling; it's creating a sacred space that captures your spiritual journey together. As you look back, you'll be amazed at how you can trace the fingerprints of God working in your relationship.

Don't hesitate to spice things up and find a routine that resonates with both of you! Maybe you'll establish a formal prayer time every morning, or perhaps you prefer the spontaneity of praying together throughout the day. The blend of both might just be the jackpot!

Whatever your style, remember that the key ingredient is consistency. The aim isn't just to squeeze in prayers; it's to weave them into the very fabric of your lives—bonding you not only with each other but also with God.

Prayer isn't about persuading God to change His mind; it's more about inviting Him into your hearts. It's where you seek guidance, align your wills, and encounter the profound power of His love. As you commit to praying together regularly, you'll find your connection deepening in ways you never imagined. Sure, the journey may have its bumps, but the rewards will be extraordinary.

So, take the leap and embrace the transformative power of prayer as a couple! As you engage in this sacred dialogue with the divine, you'll discover a wellspring of strength, wisdom, and a clearer understanding of your shared path. Those quiet moments spent in prayer become not just rituals but cherished milestones—moments of intimate communion where your hearts turn toward God. Together, you'll explore the beautiful depths of your relationship, creating a bond that flourishes with love, faith, and purpose.

Fasting and Spiritual Renewal

Fasting, often misunderstood as mere self-denial, is a powerful spiritual discipline that can profoundly enrich a couple's relationship with God and each other. It's not about deprivation, but about redirection—redirecting our focus from earthly desires to a deeper communion with the divine. When approached thoughtfully and prayerfully as a couple, fasting becomes a crucible where your faith is refined, your bond strengthened, and your intimacy with God intensified.

The essence of fasting lies in its intentional relinquishment of something—food, entertainment, social media, or even specific habits—to create space for spiritual growth. This deliberate act of self-control fosters a dependence on God, highlighting His provision and sufficiency in our lives. It's a humbling experience that reminds us of our limitations and God's boundless grace.

For couples, fasting together offers unique benefits. It creates a shared experience, a shared sacrifice, forging a deeper connection through mutual commitment. The shared journey through the discipline builds empathy, strengthens unity, and provides opportunities for deeper conversations and shared prayer. The absence of physical cravings can ironically open space for spiritual cravings, deepening the desire for God's presence and guidance.

However, approaching fasting requires careful consideration and preparation. It's not a competition, nor a race to prove spiritual prowess. The goal is not the length of the fast, but the quality of the time spent seeking God. Before embarking on this journey, honest conversations are crucial. Discuss the type of fast you'll undertake (partial or complete abstinence from food, specific foods, or other habits), its duration, and the spiritual goals you hope to achieve. Flexibility and understanding are essential; what works for one individual may not work for the other.

For instance, a partial fast, focusing on abstaining from certain foods or specific meals, can be a gentler introduction to the practice. This allows for gradual adjustment and reduces the likelihood of physical discomfort that could hinder spiritual focus. Consider a shared fast of one meal a day, or abstaining from certain things like dessert or caffeine for a week. This method reduces the physical demands and allows more energy for prayer and spiritual reflection.

A complete fast, involving abstention from all food and drink for a set period, should only be undertaken after careful consideration of your individual health and capabilities. It requires adequate preparation and, importantly, medical clearance if you have underlying health conditions. This kind of fast necessitates a profound commitment, both individually and as a couple, requiring mutual support and encouragement. It's crucial to understand that the physical discomfort is a temporary sacrifice that shouldn't overshadow the spiritual gains.

Beyond abstaining from food, consider exploring alternative forms of fasting. A "fast from technology" can provide incredible space for conversation, reflection, and deepening intimacy. A "fast from entertainment" allows for a deeper focus on spiritual reading, prayer, and service. This could involve temporarily eliminating television, social media, and leisure activities to create space for God and each other.

No matter the form the fast takes, maintaining open and honest communication throughout is crucial. Check in with each other regularly, sharing your experiences, struggles, and breakthroughs. Be patient and supportive; remember that this is a shared journey, not a solitary quest. Share your feelings, both positive and negative, recognizing that vulnerability deepens intimacy.

A key component of a spiritually fruitful fast is prayer. Consistent, heartfelt prayer during the fast should be a cornerstone of the experience. Pray for strength, guidance, and deeper spiritual understanding. Pray for each other, offering encouragement and support during any challenges. Pray for the spiritual fruits you desire to see in your lives and your marriage. Making prayer a central focus of your fast allows you to truly focus on seeking God and aligning your wills with his.

Remember that fasting isn't a magical formula for spiritual transformation. It's a tool, a means to an end, not the end itself. The aim is not to impress God but to draw closer to Him. The spiritual benefits arise from the intentional focus on God, the self-reflection, and the heightened awareness of His presence. Through this, your faith deepens, your vulnerabilities are laid bare, and your bond as a couple strengthens.

However, it's vital to acknowledge that fasting can reveal underlying issues in the relationship. During a fast, emotional vulnerabilities may surface. Be prepared to address any conflict constructively and with empathy. See these challenges not as setbacks, but as opportunities for deeper understanding and healing. The fast acts as a lens, magnifying both the strengths and weaknesses in your relationship, offering valuable insights for growth.

Consider journaling during your fast. Record your reflections, your struggles, and your experiences of God's presence. This personal record will serve as a powerful testament to your spiritual journey, providing a reference point for future reflection and growth. It also becomes a tool for sharing your experiences and emotions, creating opportunities for open and honest communication between you and your spouse.

After the fast, remember to break it slowly and gently. Returning to normal eating habits abruptly can have adverse effects. Take time to reflect on the experiences of the fast, acknowledging God's presence and guidance. Celebrate the spiritual growth you have experienced together and the deepened intimacy you've achieved. This reflective period is a crucial part of the process and a time for mutual encouragement and support.

In conclusion, fasting as a spiritual discipline for couples can be a powerful catalyst for growth, deepening intimacy with God and strengthening the bond between you. It's not about deprivation or self-flagellation, but about redirecting your focus, fostering dependence on God, and strengthening your relationship with Him and each other. Approached prayerfully, thoughtfully, and with open communication, fasting can be a transformative experience, paving the way for a deeper, more meaningful connection with God and your spouse. Embrace this spiritual discipline as a couple and witness the incredible transformation it brings to your lives and your love. Remember that this is a journey of faith, and God's grace will sustain you throughout.

Sabbath Observance and Rest

Sabbath observance, the intentional setting aside of a day for rest and worship, is a cornerstone of spiritual life, and for couples, it offers a unique opportunity to reconnect, recharge, and deepen their spiritual bond. It's not merely a day off from work; it's a sacred space carved out to cultivate intimacy with God and each other, a weekly reminder of His provision and our dependence on Him. In our busy lives, the Sabbath becomes a refuge, a sanctuary where the demands of the world fade into the background, allowing the gentle whisper of God's love to resonate deeply within our hearts.

The concept of rest goes far beyond simply ceasing physical activity. It's an overall rest—a cessation of the relentless mental and emotional demands we often subject ourselves to. It's a time to quiet the incessant chatter of our minds, to still the anxieties that often grip us, and to allow our souls to breathe. For couples, this shared rest becomes an opportunity to nurture intimacy, to engage in meaningful conversations, and to simply enjoy each other's presence without the pressures of daily routines. It's a time to reconnect not just with God, but with one another on a deeper level.

The Sabbath shouldn't be approached with a rigid, legalistic mindset. It's not about following a strict checklist of activities, but about cultivating a spirit of rest and worship. The specific practices might vary from couple to couple, but the underlying principle remains consistent: a deliberate pause, a conscious choice to prioritize God and each other above the relentless demands of the world. The focus should be on creating a space where God's presence can be experienced fully and where the couple can cultivate their relationship with Him and with each other.

The beauty of Sabbath observance lies in its adaptability. It's not a one-size-fits-all prescription; rather, it's a personalized journey of discovery. What works for one couple might not work for another. The key is to find practices that resonate deeply with your individual needs and preferences, creating a rhythm that nourishes your souls and strengthens your bond. Experiment, explore, and adapt your Sabbath practices as needed, allowing flexibility to accommodate life's ever- changing circumstances.

For some couples, the Sabbath might involve attending church services together, followed by a leisurely brunch and a quiet afternoon of reading or prayer. For others, it might mean spending the entire day in nature, hiking in the woods, picnicking by a lake, or simply enjoying the tranquility of their own backyard. The possibilities are endless, limited only by your creativity and your desire to create a meaningful, restorative experience.

I found that incorporating elements of nature into our Sabbaths has been particularly rejuvenating. Taking a long walk in the park, tending to our garden together, or simply sitting under a tree and enjoying the quiet beauty of nature has brought a sense of peace and tranquility to our lives. These moments of quiet contemplation, surrounded by God's creation, have allowed us to connect with Him on a deeper level, fostering a sense of awe and wonder.

Another effective practice you can adopt is engaging in shared creative activities. This could involve anything from painting or drawing together to listening to music, playing an instrument, or working on a collaborative project. The key is to choose activities that spark joy and creativity, fostering a sense of shared accomplishment and strengthening our bond.

Conversely, for some couples, the Sabbath might be a time for dedicated service to others. Volunteering at a local soup kitchen, visiting the elderly, or simply performing random acts of kindness can be a powerfully rewarding way to connect with God and with each other. The focus on outward service often leads to a deeper inward understanding of our shared faith and purpose. It's a beautiful way to express our gratitude for God's blessings and to share His love with those around us. This tangible act of love often becomes a powerful way to reconnect with each other, strengthening our shared values and faith.

Regardless of the specific practices you choose, consistent and intentional Sabbath observance is crucial. It's not a luxury to be indulged in only when time permits, but a necessity for spiritual and relational health. Just as our bodies need regular rest to function properly, our souls need regular time for renewal and rejuvenation. By prioritizing the Sabbath, we create a space for God to work in our lives, to deepen our relationship with Him, and to strengthen our bond as a couple.

Effective communication is essential during Sabbath observance. Take time to talk with your spouse about the type of rest that resonates with both of you. Be open to compromise and flexibility, recognizing that what works one week may not be suitable the next. The objective is to create a shared experience that enhances both your spiritual connection and your marital bond. This time of rest and rejuvenation fosters a deeper understanding and empathy between you and your spouse.

Regularly assess the effectiveness of your Sabbath practices. Are they genuinely helping you feel closer to God and to one another? Do you feel refreshed and renewed after your Sabbath observance? If not, it may be time to make some adjustments. Experiment with new practices and find what works best for both of you. Remember, the journey of practicing Sabbath is an ongoing process of discovery, faith, and self-reflection.

It's important to remember that the Sabbath is not about achieving perfection; rather, it is about striving for a deeper connection with God and with one another. There will be weeks when distractions intrude, and unexpected events disrupt your plans. That's okay. The spirit of the Sabbath is more important than rigidly adhering to a schedule. Grace and forgiveness are essential elements of this sacred time, allowing for imperfection and emphasizing the intention behind the practice.

Embrace the Sabbath as a gift, a divine appointment for rest, reflection, and renewal. It is a time to disconnect from the relentless demands of the world and reconnect with the source of all love and grace. By cultivating the practice of Sabbath observance in your relationship, you will discover that it is a powerful tool for deepening your intimacy with God and strengthening the bond between you and your spouse. This practice creates a marriage that is not only deeply personal but also profoundly spiritual.

The benefits of observing a consistent Sabbath go beyond the individual; they extend outward, improving your relationships with family, friends, and the community. A rested and rejuvenated couple is better prepared to face life's pressures, navigate challenges with grace and resilience, and show compassion and understanding toward others. The peace and tranquility developed during the Sabbath often spill over into other areas of life, creating a ripple effect of positivity and renewal.

As you observe the Sabbath, approach it with a spirit of gratitude. Take time to express thankfulness for God's blessings, the gift of your spouse, and the opportunity to rest and reconnect. A heart filled with gratitude opens itself more fully to God's presence, allowing you to experience His love and grace on a deeper level.

Let your Sabbath be a testament to your faith, a celebration of your love, and a source of constant renewal in your lives. This act of thanksgiving transforms the Sabbath from just a day of rest into a deeply meaningful spiritual practice.

Mentorship and Spiritual Countability

Cultivating a God-centered marriage is not a journey you take alone. Although the intimacy between husband and wife is deeply personal and sacred, seeking mentorship and spiritual accountability from other mature Christian couples can provide invaluable benefits. Consider it an additional layer to the rich tapestry of your faith journey—one that is woven with the wisdom, experience, and unwavering support of fellow travelers on the same path.

Just as a seasoned athlete benefits from a skilled coach who provides guidance and feedback, couples can thrive under the watchful eye and encouraging words of a mature, spiritually grounded couple. This kind of mentorship is not about seeking perfection or pointing out faults; rather, it focuses on gaining perspective, receiving encouragement, and learning from the experiences of others who have navigated similar challenges in their own marriages. Such mentors can offer invaluable insights, helping you identify blind spots, navigate difficult situations, and ultimately grow closer to both God and each other.

Finding the right mentors isn't about looking for perfect individuals; it's about identifying couples who embody the qualities you admire and wish to cultivate in your own relationship. Seek out couples who demonstrate deep faith, a strong and loving marriage, and a willingness to share their wisdom and experiences. They are not your judges but your fellow travelers, sharing the journey with you. You can find these individuals within your church community, through small group studies, or even within your broader circle of friends and family.

Approaching potential mentors requires humility and a genuine desire to learn. Start by expressing your admiration for their relationship and your aspiration to grow spiritually as a couple. Clearly explain what you hope to gain from the mentorship, being upfront about your needs and expectations. A simple, heartfelt conversation can lead to a deeply rewarding relationship. This process is not about overwhelming them with your problems; rather, it focuses on seeking guidance, learning from their example, and fostering mutual growth.

The process of accountability is essential. Mentorship offers guidance, while accountability ensures that you are responsible for applying that guidance in your life. Choosing a couple to hold you accountable requires a significant level of trust and vulnerability, as you will be sharing the most intimate aspects of your marriage and seeking their loving support. This accountability is not punitive; rather, it is supportive and constructive. It aims to create a safe space where you can openly share your struggles and celebrate your victories, knowing that you have a support system to help you navigate challenges.

Accountability partners can offer encouragement when you face challenges and celebrate your successes when you overcome obstacles. They provide a different perspective, a listening ear, and supportive advice. They serve as a gentle reminder to stay on track with your spiritual goals and as a cheering squad when you make progress. This relationship is reciprocal, where both individuals benefit from sharing their journey of faith.

How can you effectively implement spiritual mentorship and accountability in your relationship? Consider holding regular meetings—perhaps monthly or quarterly—to discuss your spiritual journey as a couple. These meetings can include prayer, sharing of scripture, discussing challenges, and celebrating victories together.

Open communication is essential. Be honest about your struggles, successes, and aspirations. Avoid becoming defensive; instead, view constructive feedback as an opportunity for growth. Remember, these meetings are not therapy sessions but rather opportunities for spiritual growth and encouragement, guided by the wisdom and experiences of others.

The role of prayer is essential during this process. Make it a point to pray together with your mentors, asking for God's guidance and wisdom as you prepare for your marriage. Also, take time to pray for your mentors, expressing your gratitude for their support and guidance. Prayer serves as the foundation that strengthens your relationship with them and provides a spiritual base for your ongoing journey together.

A practical approach could be to focus on a specific area of your relationship during each meeting. For example, one meeting might concentrate on improving communication skills, another on deepening prayer habits, and another on managing conflict constructively. This structured method keeps your meetings focused and ensures that you address particular needs within your relationship.

Remember, the relationship with your mentors is not about dependence; it is about mutual support and encouragement. It is a partnership built on shared faith and a desire to grow closer to God. As you learn from them, you will also find opportunities to offer support and encouragement in return. Your growth becomes their growth, creating a powerful synergy of faith and fellowship.

The benefits of mentorship and accountability extend beyond your individual relationship. As you grow closer to God, you will naturally overflow with His love, sharing it with others within your community. Your example can inspire other couples to embark on their own spiritual journeys, creating a ripple effect of transformation within your church and beyond. Your strengthened faith provides a foundation for service and acts of kindness, extending your reach into the wider world.

Maintaining open and honest communication is essential for a successful mentoring relationship. It's important to share your needs and expectations with your mentor and to seek clarification whenever necessary. A healthy mentoring relationship is built on mutual respect, understanding, and a shared desire for spiritual growth.

Additionally, remember that even the most experienced mentors face their own struggles and challenges. They are not perfect, but their willingness to share their vulnerabilities makes their guidance even more valuable. They can teach you that it's okay to stumble, that growth is a journey, and that God's grace is always sufficient. Embrace their imperfections; they are evidence of a genuine faith journey. Learn from their successes, as well as from their mistakes. This overall approach will give you a well-rounded understanding of how to navigate the complexities of a deeply spiritual marriage. The journey is ongoing—a continuous process of learning, growing, and deepening your relationship with God and with each other.

CHAPTER 5

BUILDING A STRONG SPIRITUAL COMMUNITY

The foundation of a God-centered marriage isn't built solely within the walls of a home; it thrives and flourishes within the vibrant community of a local church. Imagine it like this: just as individual branches draw life from the roots of a mighty tree, a couple finds nourishment and unwavering support amidst the fellowship of believers. It's more than just attending Sunday services; it's about diving headfirst into the life of the church, getting involved in its various ministries, and seizing the opportunities for spiritual growth and mutual encouragement that are waiting for you.

The church is far more than a mere building—it's a living, breathing organism, the body of Christ, where every member plays a vital role. Getting actively involved means way more than just warming a pew; it calls for a conscious effort to connect with others, to serve generously, and to keep your hearts open to being served in return. This commitment fosters a strong sense of belonging, strengthens bonds of fellowship, and creates a nurturing environment where you can joyfully share your triumphs and candidly express your struggles.

One of the most remarkable gifts of engaging deeply with your church community is the rich network of spiritual mentors and accountability partners it offers. In the congregation, you'll meet individuals and couples who've navigated similar paths, faced similar challenges, and are eager to share their wisdom and support. They're not perfect; they're fellow travelers on this journey, ready to offer encouragement and share lessons learned from their own lives. Their insights, often forged through years of faithful living, can save you from some pitfalls and fast-track your spiritual growth.

Consider joining a small group Bible study. These intimate settings are gold mines for deeper connections and genuine fellowship. They create the perfect environment to share your thoughts, feelings, and struggles openly, all without the fear of judgment. Engaging in shared study of scriptures promotes spiritual growth, and the open dialogue within the group provides a safe space for vulnerability and mutual support. In these small groups, you'll find encouragement, accountability, and an undeniable sense of belonging that can enrich your relationship. Together, embarking on this shared faith journey not only deepens your individual spiritual walks but also strengthens your commitment to each other.

Engaging in your church community offers an incredible opportunity to deepen not only your relationship with God but also the bond you share as a couple. Imagine the joy of volunteering together in a ministry—whether that means working with children, helping the elderly, or participating in a community outreach program. Each moment spent serving is a chance to express your love for God and for one another, while also enriching your marriage through selfless acts of compassion.

But it doesn't stop there! Church events like retreats, conferences, and social gatherings create the perfect atmosphere for fellowship. These occasions are all about connection—where you can meet other couples who share your faith, share laughs, and create unforgettable memories together. The friendships you forge during these experiences can blossom into lifelong support systems, providing encouragement and camaraderie as you navigate your spiritual journeys side by side.

Remember, active participation isn't about putting on a show; it's about authenticity and open-hearted engagement. It's the little things—showing up, being present, and allowing yourselves to be vulnerable—that truly enrich your connection to one another and your church community. Embrace the uniqueness of each person you meet, knowing that everyone is on their own spiritual path. Offer a listening ear, a helping hand, or simply a warm smile—these gestures can foster a culture of grace and understanding.

Don't underestimate the power of prayer within your church community. Engaging in prayer for your church, its leaders, and fellow members isn't just an obligation; it's a demonstration of love and a transformative experience. When you intercede for others, you bolster your relationship with God and your fellow believers. This act of service connects you deeply to the spiritual fabric of your church, enhancing its overall health and vitality.

As you pray together and for others, you contribute to a powerful collective force that unites your community in faith. Your shared experiences and heartfelt prayers become the threads that weave your stories together—a beautiful testament to your journey as a couple within the embrace of your church family.

Getting involved in your local church is about so much more than just showing up on Sundays. It's an exciting opportunity to dive into a community that can really transform your life. Supporting your church financially isn't just about giving money; it's about backing a mission that helps the church grow and make a difference in the neighborhood.

But giving isn't all about cash. Think about sharing your unique talents, putting in some volunteer hours, and looking for ways to lift up those around you. This kind of generosity not only boosts your faith but also strengthens your marriage and deepens your connections with God and your community.

And let's not forget the little things—the warmth of belonging, the encouragement you get during tough times, and the joy of celebrating milestones with people who get what you're going through. Your church can be a refuge, a place where you find connection with others who are navigating life's ups and downs, offering invaluable support along the way.

A strong church community brings so much value. It's where acceptance thrives and support is always around—the perfect space to feel God's love. You can share your faith and find the strength to tackle any challenges that come your way. This sense of belonging not only lifts you but also strengthens your marriage, providing that extra cushion during life's storms. A relationship grounded in faith flourishes in an environment like this, surrounded by support that nurtures both partners.

Think of your church as a living, breathing community—always growing and changing. Every person plays a part, contributing their gifts and being celebrated as a valuable member of God's family. Getting involved adds more color and texture to the community, making it richer and more diverse. It's a two-way street; you gain support while giving back, enhancing the spiritual experiences of everyone involved.

Finding the right church can feel like uncovering a treasure on your spiritual journey. Look for a place that aligns with your beliefs and feels comfortable, where you can meet others who share your passion for faith. Don't rush into anything; take your time visiting different churches until you find one that feels just right. Trust that

God will lead you to a community where you'll really grow and thrive.

Once you've found your church home, jump in with both feet! Join a small group, get involved in a ministry, attend events, and, most importantly, lift up your church family in prayer. The more you engage, the more it will enrich your spiritual life, strengthen your marriage, and contribute to the church's health. By getting involved, you'll see firsthand how powerful a supportive spiritual community can be, laying down a solid foundation for a God-centered marriage that stands the test of time.

This isn't just an obligation; it's a fantastic opportunity to be part of something bigger than yourself. Together, you'll create a cozy, supportive community that will uplift both your lives and the lives of those around you for years to come. It's a meaningful investment in your faith, your marriage, and the people in your life. So, take that leap and embrace the amazing journey ahead!

Serving in Ministry Together

Serving alongside your spouse in ministry can be one of the most enriching experiences of your life, transforming both your relationship and your shared faith in ways you might never have imagined. It goes beyond merely adding another task to your busy schedules; it's about joining forces to engage in God's work, weaving your love and commitment into the very fabric of His Kingdom.

Imagine the joy of facing challenges together, turning them into opportunities for growth. Picture disagreements evolving into refined teamwork, and celebrations blossoming into moments of profound shared joy. It's a powerful testament to partnership, reflecting the essence of Gog

God – Father, Son, and Holy Ghost working together in perfect harmony as one.

Think about the parable of the vineyard workers. In this story, each worker, regardless of the hour they began, received the same reward. It beautifully illustrates that every contribution holds equal value, no matter how small or large. In a shared ministry, you and your spouse bring your unique gifts and talents to the table, creating a union that's far greater than the sum of your efforts. This is not a competition; it's a dynamic collaboration, recognizing and utilizing each other's strengths while accommodating each other's weaknesses to achieve something truly remarkable.

For instance, what if one of you has a knack for teaching while the other excels at organization? Together, you could lead a vibrant Sunday school class, with one crafting engaging lessons that inspire the children and the other handling logistics to ensure everything runs smoothly. The sense of accomplishment that comes from this shared success will not only strengthen your bond but will also serve as a tangible symbol of your teamwork and dedication to God. It's a practical demonstration of love, both for each other and for those you serve, turning shared effort into a collective joy—a reflection of your spiritual unity.

Or consider a couple who shares a passion for hospitality. Opening their home for fellowship gatherings could create a warm, inviting atmosphere for other couples in the church community. Their collaborative planning, preparation, and hosting foster genuine connections and build strong relationships. In these moments— serving food, sharing stories, and offering a comforting presence— they create profound expressions of shared faith, significantly contributing to the spiritual well-being of others. They are actively building the Kingdom, not just participating in it.

So, as you navigate your journey together, remember: your shared service in ministry is not just about what you do; it's about who you are becoming together. Celebrate the unique gift of partnership as you walk hand in hand, serving and growing in faith side by side.

The possibilities for serving together as a couple are as diverse and colorful as the unique gifts and talents that God has generously bestowed upon each of us. Imagine the joy of connecting with one another while diving into meaningful activities! Whether it's helping out in the church nursery, lending a hand with the youth group, volunteering at a local soup kitchen, leading a vibrant Bible study, or organizing an exciting church event, these opportunities invite you to work side by side, sharing in both the challenges and the rewards. The secret? Discover where your shared passions align with the needs in your community. Finding that sweet spot will take a bit of prayerful reflection, some honest conversations, and a brave willingness to step outside your comfort zones.

Serving together also opens the door to powerful conflict resolution. Let's face it, disagreements are part of any relationship! However, navigating these discussions within the context of shared ministry can transform them into moments of spiritual growth. Instead of letting conflicts become stumbling blocks, think of them as stepping stones to greater understanding. You'll learn to compromise, empathize, and approach differences with humility. When your focus shifts from individual desires to the collective goal of serving God and others, it lightens the load of disagreements and fosters a deeper respect for each other's perspectives.

Moreover, shared ministry has a remarkable way of deepening intimacy and understanding. Picture this: You and your spouse collaborating on a project, facing challenges together, and celebrating milestones as a team. This kind of partnership creates an unbreakable bond. You'll get to see each other's strengths and weaknesses in action, learning to rely on one another and developing a profound appreciation for each other's contributions. These shared experiences unveil facets of each other's character and spiritual maturity that might otherwise remain hidden, transforming your relationship into something truly extraordinary.

And let's not forget the ripple effect of your shared service! Your commitment and collaboration can inspire those around you, shining a light on the transformative power of faith and the strength of a God-centered marriage. When others witness your unwavering devotion to serving God together, it can motivate them to deepen their own faith and pursue more meaningful relationships with God. You become living proof that serving together isn't just an ideal; it's a beautiful reality filled with purpose and fulfillment.

So, remember, this shared service goes beyond just ticking off tasks. It's about embodying your faith as a dynamic team, reflecting the loving nature of God's grace. It's a powerful expression of your commitment to each other and your shared calling. Serving together is not about being perfect; it's about wholeheartedly giving your time, talents, and hearts to God's work. Embrace the imperfections, the challenges, and the disagreements, for they'll become opportunities for growth, forging a stronger bond and a richer understanding of your shared spiritual journey.

The journey of serving together in ministry is truly a marathon, not a sprint. It's so much more than just checking off tasks; it's about fostering a culture of commitment, reveling in the small acts of service that often go unnoticed, and joyfully celebrating every victory, no matter how small.

Think of it this way: each challenge you face together is an opportunity for growth, a chance to deepen your partnership. Embrace those hurdles with grace and understanding—they can lead to the most profound moments of connection.

As you embark on this incredible journey, keep in mind the essentials: prayer, communication, and unwavering mutual support. These aren't just buzzwords; they are the very foundation of a successful and fulfilling ministry. Regularly seek guidance through prayer, communicate with sincerity and openness, and always be there for one another. Together, hand in hand, you're tending to God's vineyard, and the rewards are beyond measure.

Imagine the positive impact you can have on the lives of others, the relationships you will build, and the love you will spread. It's a beautiful testament to the power of faith when lived out in unity—a reflection of God's love shining brightly in the world.

So, as you navigate this journey together, remember: it's not just about the destination. The journey itself is a blessing, filled with moments that reveal the enduring strength of a God-centered life lived in partnership and service. Embrace every moment, and let it inspire you to make a difference!

Participating in Small Groups

Joining a small group isn't just about showing up for a meeting; it's a beautiful journey of connecting and intertwining with a community that truly understands the unique joys and challenges of a faith-filled marriage. Picture yourselves not as isolated islands, but as vibrant threads woven into a rich, interconnected tapestry. This is the incredible power of belonging—a strength that springs from shared experiences and mutual encouragement.

Think about the parable of the shepherd and his sheep. Each sheep is known and cared for individually; the shepherd leads them to lush green pastures, protects them from harm, and guides them with unwavering love. In a small group, you find that same nurturing spirit, that same sense of belonging and personal attention that can sometimes be lost in larger congregations. You're not just a face in the crowd; you are a cherished part of a loving flock.

In the whirlwind of everyday life, it's easy to feel disconnected—even when surrounded by fellow churchgoers. The demands of work, family, and personal responsibilities can leave us starved for deeper connections, those relationships that nourish us spiritually and emotionally. A small group offers a sanctuary, a welcoming space to relax, share your vulnerabilities, and find the support you need to navigate life's ups and downs.

In this close-knit setting, you'll meet couples who truly understand your journey. They've faced similar struggles, celebrated victories with you, and walked through the challenges of marriage with a shared commitment to faith. This common ground creates a special kinship, transcending superficial interactions. It's a place where authenticity thrives—a space where vulnerability is celebrated, and you can share your struggles freely, without fear of judgment.

The benefits of small groups extend well beyond emotional support. They also offer powerful opportunities for spiritual growth and accountability. Through engaging Bible studies, profound discussions, and heartfelt prayers, you'll deepen your understanding of God's word and strengthen your commitment to living a life that honors Him. You'll be encouraged to stretch your faith, step out of your comfort zones, and embrace the life-changing power of God's grace. With accountability partners woven into the fabric of your small group, you'll find gentle nudges back onto the right path during moments of doubt or weakness, providing the encouragement and guidance we all need.

Imagine this: you're sitting in a cozy room filled with warm laughter and familiar faces, sharing your struggles with infertility, the pressures of parenting in a rapidly changing world, or the delicate balance of work and family life. In this intimate group, these aren't just isolated issues; they transform into shared experiences that weave a powerful sense of unity and understanding.

Picture the warmth that envelops you when you hear stories from others who have walked similar paths, offering not just comfort but also hope and practical advice. It's a reminder that you're not alone in your struggles and that God's grace is more than sufficient, even during the darkest of times. In these moments, you discover the strength that comes from shared vulnerability—real connections forged through honesty.

And let's not forget the joy! Whether it's the joyous announcement of a new baby, landing that dream job, or wrapping up a challenging project, every victory becomes an opportunity for celebration. The group bursts into a heartfelt chorus of praise, enriching your achievements with a profound sense of community. Your joy grows exponentially when shared, and those blessings feel even more meaningful.

But finding the right small group? That's key. Seek a group whose values resonate with yours, where you can truly be yourselves and speak candidly about your journeys. Don't hesitate to explore a few different groups until you find the one that feels just right. Prayerfully consider your options, ask trusted friends or your pastor for recommendations, and above all, trust your intuition. The right group will feel like family—a supportive network that nurtures your spiritual and personal growth.

Think about what's most important to you and your partner. Are you drawn to a group centered around Bible study, prayer, or just fellowship? Do you prefer a structured approach or a laid-back, informal vibe? A large gathering or a smaller, more intimate setting? These are crucial questions that will help guide your decision.

Once you find a group that feels like home, commit to being a regular part of it. Consistency is everything when it comes to building strong relationships and realizing all that the group can offer. Remember, this is a two-way street. Your insights, contributions, and service will enrich the group just as much as you'll be nurtured by it.

Moreover, a small group offers an incredible chance to serve others together. Think about the impact you can make through community outreach projects, volunteering your time and talents to better the lives of those around you. This shared service not only strengthens the bond between you as a couple but deepens your faith and expresses love for God and all of humanity. Just think of the miracle of the loaves and fishes—small contributions, faith, and a shared intention can create impactful change.

Beyond the immediate benefits, consider the deeper connections you'll cultivate. Sharing your spiritual journey with another couple fosters intimacy and vulnerability in your relationship. Together, you navigate life's complexities—the ups and downs—as a united front, learning to appreciate each other's strengths and weaknesses. It's a beautiful embodiment of walking together on a shared spiritual path.

Ultimately, participating in a small group is not just an obligation; it's a meaningful investment in community and spiritual growth. It's where the promises of encouragement, guidance, and the transformative power of faith come alive. It's about finding a place where you can share your joys and struggles, strengthen the bonds of your marriage, and carve out an enduring legacy of faith and love.

If your church community doesn't offer this small group, you could suggest that you and your spouse start one together through prayer and permission from God. Talk to your pastor, and have them help you pray on this matter, too. It is a much-needed support system that is rarely offered but greatly needed.

Supporting Missions and Global Outreach

Our journey of faith is an adventure that goes far beyond the four walls of our church or the comfort of our homes. It truly takes flight when we let our love and compassion spill over into the wider world, reaching those in need across the globe. Supporting missions and global outreach isn't just a noble endeavor; it's a vital thread in the tapestry of a faith-filled life—a living testament to the transformative power of God's love in action. It's a chance for us to put our faith into motion, creating ripples of grace that extend far beyond our own shores.

Take a moment to reflect on the parable of the Good Samaritan. He didn't limit his compassion to his own people or hometown; he reached out to a stranger who was in desperate need. His selfless act transcended cultural boundaries and became a stunning symbol of God's boundless love. Similarly, when we get involved in missions and global outreach, we participate in God's redemptive work in the world, becoming instruments of His grace and compassion. This outward expression of faith not only transforms the lives of those we serve but also deepens our spiritual connection with God. Each act of giving, stretching beyond our comfort zones, cultivates a deep sense of humility and gratitude within us.

There are countless ways to get involved with mission activities, each providing unique opportunities for spiritual growth and commitment to God's work. Consider the incredible impact of financial support. Even a modest, regular contribution can make a world of difference, supplying essential resources for missionaries, backing community development projects, and providing relief during crises. Your generosity becomes a beacon of God's love, offering sustenance, hope, and opportunities to those who need it most.

Remember, every gift, no matter how small, is a seed of faith planted in fertile ground. God takes our offerings and multiplies them in miraculous ways, leading to positive change across the world. Don't underestimate the power of your generosity; it's not just a transaction but a potent force for good, a catalyst for transformation, and a profound expression of your unwavering faith.

But let's not forget the remarkable power of prayer. Interceding for missionaries, those serving in impoverished communities, and individuals facing persecution for their beliefs is a crucial act of spiritual warfare. Our prayers transform into a formidable weapon in God's arsenal, granting strength, courage, and protection to those on the front lines of His kingdom. It's a silent yet powerful force, revealing our steadfast faith and commitment to standing alongside our brothers and sisters in Christ.

Imagine the power of a unified prayer group, lifting up the names of missionaries, pleading for the salvation of souls, and interceding for the world in need. This shared prayer becomes a beautiful symphony of faith—hearts and voices united in a common cause. It's a vibrant expression of community, a testament to the strength found in unity, and a magnificent catalyst for spiritual growth both individually and collectively.

Have you ever considered the incredible impact that service can have on your life and the lives of others? Imagine stepping into a world where your hands are calloused, but your heart is bursting with joy—where every action you take is a testament to faith and love. Short-term mission trips offer an invaluable opportunity to dive headfirst into God's work, allowing you to witness the challenges and triumphs of ministry up close.

Picture yourself in a remote village, tirelessly building a school, sharing the Gospel with eager listeners, or providing much-needed medical care to those who are suffering. Yes, the conditions may be tough and the challenges very real, but the rewards? They are beyond measure. When you return home, you don't just carry stories; you return transformed, with a renewed appreciation for your own blessings and a deeper sense of purpose. You become not just a witness, but a living testament to the transformative power of God's love and grace.

But you don't have to travel halfway across the world to make a difference. Even in your own community, there are countless ways to serve. Support local organizations that collaborate with international missions, join fundraising events, or volunteer to lend your time and talents to missionary efforts right at home. You could be packaging food for the needy, organizing clothing drives, or rallying your community to raise awareness for vital mission causes. Each little act of service, no matter how small it seems, is a powerful expression of God's love—showing your commitment to extending His grace and compassion wherever it's needed most.

Think creatively! What unique gifts do you have that can support mission efforts? Are you a whiz with words or a talented graphic designer? Why not create engaging materials for missionaries and organizations? An artist or musician? Use your creativity to inspire and uplift those around you. Every skill you possess can be a tool for furthering God's kingdom and spreading His love to a world that craves connection.

But don't stop at individual contributions—think about the powerful impact that comes from working together. Collaborate with your church or local community to organize mission trips, fundraising efforts, or awareness campaigns. When you join forces, your combined efforts create a powerful synergy—amplifying your impact and reaching far beyond what you could accomplish alone.

Engaging in missions and global outreach isn't merely about helping others; it's an enriching part of your spiritual journey. It's about experiencing the transformative power of God's love firsthand and realizing the role you can play in His divine plan. It pushes you beyond your comfort zone, expands your horizons, and deepens your understanding of your place in this vast tapestry of God's work.

Consider the ripple effect of your actions—a simple act of kindness, a heartfelt prayer, or a modest contribution can spark a chain reaction of positive change, reaching people you may never even meet. Your involvement becomes a radiant demonstration of your faith, shining bright in a world that sometimes feels overwhelmingly dark.

The spiritual rewards of supporting missions and global outreach are profound. You'll find a sense of purpose, experience deepened faith, and discover an expanded capacity for love—all while forging a deeper connection with God through service. It's an investment in the kingdom of God, creating a legacy of love that reaches far beyond your lifetime.

So why wait? Embrace the opportunity that awaits you; the blessings are just waiting to be discovered. Your faith journey extends beyond your doorstep and your community, stretching across the globe—a beautiful testament to the boundless love and compassion of God. Answer this call, and let your faith blossom in the fertile soil of global outreach.

When it comes to deciding which missions to support, prayer is essential for gaining knowledge. It can be daunting to see so many televised missions that have turned out to be fraudulent. However, televised missions are not the only options available; there are many local missions as well. The most important factor is being obedient to God. Simply ask Him—He will guide you to the missions where He wants you to support and work in the mission field.

CHAPTER 6

UNDERSTANDING GOD'S LOVE IN MARRIAGE

The unwavering love of God, a boundless ocean of grace and mercy, stands as the ultimate example for marital love. It's a love that doesn't waver, doesn't falter, and doesn't demand perfection. It's a love that sees our flaws, our imperfections, and our failings, yet chooses to embrace us nonetheless. This unconditional love, so freely given, is the bedrock upon which a truly fulfilling and God-centered marriage is built. Understanding this divine model profoundly transforms our understanding of what it means to love and be loved within the marital bond.

Think about the nature of God's love as depicted in scripture. He relentlessly pursues us, even when we stray. Time and again, He forgives, offering us fresh starts and clean slates. His love isn't a currency to be earned but a freely given gift—an expression of His infinite compassion. This reality isn't merely a theological concept; it's a transformative force that can redefine our marital relationships and expectations.

When we embrace the understanding of God's love, it fundamentally changes our expectations in marriage. We move beyond conditional love—a type of love that depends on performance, achievement, or the fulfillment of certain expectations. Instead, we enter a space where love is not reliant on our partner's perfection. Rather, it is rooted in a steadfast commitment to cherish and support them unconditionally. This is a love that celebrates our partner's strengths while gracefully navigating their weaknesses.

This statement does not mean that we condone harmful behaviors or accept mistreatment. On the contrary, a God-centered marriage requires both partners to actively work toward personal growth and spiritual maturity. It does, however, mean that our love is not threatened by imperfections, disagreements, or occasional failures. Instead, we should approach conflict with grace, forgiveness, and a desire for reconciliation, reflecting the forgiving heart of God Himself.

Every marriage faces challenges—disagreements, frustrations, and moments that test our bond. But when our love is grounded in God's unwavering affection, these challenges become stepping stones for growth and deeper understanding. They are opportunities to learn how to navigate conflict through prayer, seeking divine guidance, and practicing forgiveness.

Now, consider the incredible power of forgiveness—an act that beautifully reflects God's own unconditional love. It requires humility and empathy; it's an active choice to release resentment and allow healing to take root. Forgiveness is not simply a passive acceptance of wrongs but a transformative action that can revitalize our relationships. When we forgive, we experience God's grace in profound ways, healing not just past wounds but also paving the way for a strong, resilient future together.

In the beautiful tapestry of marriage, communication stands out as a vibrant thread, woven intricately under the guiding light of God's unconditional love. Picture this: when we engage in conversation with our partner, approaching each exchange with genuine love and understanding, we create a sacred space—a nurturing haven for vulnerability and intimacy. Here, honesty blooms, trust deepens, and the emotional bond between us is fortified. It's a dance of hearts, where each word spoken is a step closer to one another.

Now, let's talk about prayer. Imagine the power of coming together in shared prayer, a vital practice in a God-centered marriage. This isn't just a routine; it's a magical moment when our hearts and souls unite in pursuit of something greater—God's will for us. In those moments of lifting our voices together, we find strength, comfort, and the divine guidance we need to weather life's storms. Inviting God into our marriage isn't just a ritual, it's a way of embracing His wisdom and finding clarity in the chaos of daily life.

Acknowledging God's unconditional love also empowers us to embrace our imperfections. Let's face it: we will stumble and fall; nobody's perfect. But it's not about avoiding mistakes—it's about growing from them. Just like we seek forgiveness from God, we must also extend that grace to ourselves and our spouses. By fostering self-compassion, we create an atmosphere of acceptance and humility, allowing forgiveness to flow naturally between us. When we forgive ourselves, we wield the power to forgive our partner, reinforcing the love we share.

Understanding our unique strengths and weaknesses is another beautiful aspect of a God-centered marriage. Each of us is gifted with unique talents that, when celebrated, form a powerful synergy. Together, we can achieve our common goals, build a loving family, and faithfully serve God. Imagine harnessing your distinct strengths, working side by side, and creating a life that reflects God's love—what a powerful partnership!

When conflicts arise, and they inevitably will, our understanding of God's unconditional love guides us toward constructive resolution.

Instead of letting anger or accusation cloud our judgment, we approach disagreements with humility and a desire to understand. Listening to each other's perspectives, even when they differ from our own, respects the bond we share. With prayer, we seek guidance, allowing God's wisdom to illuminate our path toward resolution. This process not only deepens our respect for one another but also strengthens our connection and communication.

The grace we find in God's love extends beautifully into our daily lives—it's in those little acts of kindness, the sweet gestures that say "I'm thinking of you," and the unwavering commitment to prioritize each other's needs. It's in shared laughter and quiet moments of companionship, building a life hand in hand through both joy and sorrow. These everyday interactions cultivate a rich intimacy that deepens our bond, reminding us that love thrives in the details.

Even amid life's profound challenges—be it illness, grief, or financial strain—God's love continues to be our anchor. Through pain and crisis, His unwavering presence offers us strength and resilience. In those trying times, we lean on each other, draw upon our shared faith, and cling to the promise that God will never abandon us. Together, we become a source of support, encouraging one another and fortifying our connection through faith.

Ultimately, experiencing the abundance of God's love in our marriage inspires us to share that gift with the world. Our relationship transforms into a living testimony of God's grace, serving as a beacon for others on their journey to a God-centered marriage. By embodying love, compassion, and support for those around us, we enrich not only our own lives but also the bond we share with one another.

This journey—a daily exploration of faith—reveals the beauty and strength that flourish when marriage is built upon the foundation of

God's unconditional love. It's an adventure of loving freely and renewing that love endlessly, transforming our lives and crafting our marriage into a beautiful reflection of His boundless grace.

Reflecting God's Love to Each Other

Reflecting God's boundless love within marriage is not just about understanding a concept; it's an exciting, daily adventure filled with purposeful actions, heartfelt words, and resolute attitudes. Each day, we have the opportunity to actively embody God's character in our relationships, showcasing His unwavering grace, limitless forgiveness, and relentless love. Imagine stepping beyond the limitations of conditional love—where affection is tied to performance—and embracing a love that is freely given, no matter the circumstances.

Think about the parable of the Good Samaritan. Here's a figure who defied societal norms, showing compassion and selflessness to a stranger in dire need. This act of radical love isn't just a story; it's a challenge for us to extend that same compassion and understanding within our marriages. It's about reaching out to our spouse with kindness, even when they stumble, and being there not out of obligation, but with genuine care for their well-being. It's a commitment to prioritize their needs alongside our own, ensuring that the health and happiness of our relationship comes first.

Reflecting God's love is intricately woven into our everyday lives. It's found in those little gestures—the unexpected cup of coffee in bed, the sweet note on the bathroom mirror, or the willingness to tackle a household chore, even when our energy is running low. These small, intentional acts carry immense weight; they declare the depth of our commitment and the authenticity of our affection. They lay the foundation for trust, intimacy, and security, all essential pillars of a vibrant, God-centered marriage.

99

Words are just as powerful in manifesting God's love. Let's choose kindness, affirmation, and encouragement to uplift our partner, nurturing their spirit and creating a loving atmosphere. Instead of allowing criticism to creep in, let's fill our conversations with grace and understanding. When tension arises—and it will—let's strive to see things from our spouse's viewpoint, actively listening to their feelings, even if we don't fully agree. Responding with empathy rather than defensiveness can transform conflict into a growth opportunity, fostering a space where both partners feel safe, valued, and understood.

Forgiveness, too, plays a crucial role in our pursuit of reflecting God's love. Just as He consistently forgives our missteps, we should willingly extend that same forgiveness to our spouse, over and over again. This doesn't mean we have to excuse hurtful actions; instead, it's about letting go of resentment, bitterness, and anger to allow healing to flourish. Choosing grace over judgment, love over retribution, is vital. It requires humility and the courage to acknowledge our own imperfections, helping us to rebuild trust and connection. Forgiveness isn't just a gift to our partner; it's also a loving act of self-care, allowing us to free ourselves from the burdens of negativity and hurt, fostering a healthier relationship for both.

Reflecting God's love in marriage is a beautiful and enriching journey that transforms both partners. Imagine a relationship where selfless service becomes the heartbeat of your daily lives—a space where putting each other's needs first becomes second nature. It's not just about the grand gestures, but the sweet, everyday moments: waking up just a little earlier to surprise your spouse with breakfast, running errands to lighten their load, or simply being there to listen during tough times. These acts of kindness create a tapestry of love that lifts both of you.

As we navigate life together, it's vital to cultivate gratitude. In the hustle and bustle, it's easy to overlook the incredible blessings our spouses bring to our lives. Taking a moment to express appreciation for their efforts, love, and the simple joy of their presence strengthens your bond. Think about the last time you verbally acknowledged something your partner did. Remember how it felt? Those moments of gratitude deepen your affection and remind you both of the beautiful partnership you share.

Respect is another essential thread in the fabric of a loving marriage. Every individual brings unique perspectives and passions to the table. Honor those differences! Embracing each other's individuality fosters a nurturing environment where both partners feel secure and cherished. It's about valuing your partner's opinions, even when they differ from yours. After all, a relationship built on respect allows both partners to thrive, growing stronger together.

Intimacy is so much more than physical closeness; it's about merging hearts, minds, and souls. Imagine walking hand in hand through life's challenges while pursuing spiritual growth together. Physical intimacy—when rooted in respect and love—becomes a sacred expression of your connection, reflecting the divine union God envisioned. It should be approached with tenderness, nurturing the emotional and spiritual ties you've built.

Engaging in shared prayer and spiritual practices is another powerful way to reflect God's love. Imagine sitting down together, talking to God about your hopes, dreams, and fears. Praying as a couple not only strengthens your faith but also creates a sense of spiritual intimacy and unity that can weather life's storms. This shared journey of faith guides you both, reminding you that you're in this together, supported by the divine.

Lastly, never underestimate the power of embracing each other's strengths and differences. God has designed each of us with unique talents and gifts, making us stronger together. Celebrating these differences rather than trying to change one another enriches your relationship in ways you may not have imagined. By leveraging each other's strengths, you'll achieve incredible things you could never do alone.

Remember, reflecting God's love in marriage isn't a one-time achievement. It's a continuous adventure filled with growth and discovery. It requires commitment, an openness to learn, and a willingness to choose grace, forgiveness, and compassion every day. As you embrace this journey, you'll celebrate the beauty of a love that mirrors the boundless love of God—a love that invites you both to become the best versions of yourselves. With unwavering devotion, your marriage can bloom into a vibrant reflection of divine love, showcasing the strength and elegance that comes from a deep, committed partnership.

Forgiving as Christ Forgave

Forgiveness, as we've touched upon, is not merely a desirable trait in a God-centered marriage; it's the bedrock of a strong and lasting relationship. Think about it: forgiveness mirrors God's endless mercy—an incredible grace granted to us, even when we stumble time and again. When we forgive as Christ forgave, we're making a deliberate choice to embrace love over bitterness, grace over judgment, and healing over resentment. It's not just a one-time act; it's a daily commitment, a spiritual practice that calls for humility and compassion.

Now, let's pause for a moment and consider what unforgiveness does to us. Picture it like lugging around a hefty stone—each day it gets heavier, weighing us down. Unforgiveness festers like a wound, poisoning not just our relationships but also our hearts. It clouds our judgment, distorts our perspective, and blurs our vision, making it difficult to appreciate our spouse, even when they struggle with their own flaws. This bitterness breeds resentment and anger, erecting a massive wall between partners that can feel impossible to break down. It obstructs the flow of love and trust, stifling that vital intimacy essential for a thriving marriage.

Christ's model of forgiveness was nothing short of revolutionary. It wasn't conditional or based on whether we met certain standards; it was a free gift, an extraordinary act of grace extended to us in our unworthiness. He didn't wait for us to tick off boxes of "good behavior" before forgiving us. His love was radical and unconditional, changing the course of history. This is the example we should aim to embody in our own marriages.

To forgive like Christ requires deep understanding of God's nature. It means recognizing our shared humanity and the imperfections we all carry. We are all beautifully flawed, capable of hurting those we love the most. Acknowledging this vulnerability in ourselves and our partners paves the way for compassion. It helps us approach our spouse's mistakes with grace, not judgment, and extends a hand of understanding rather than condemnation. In this way, we not only learn to forgive, but we also deepen our love and connection—a journey well worth taking.

Let's explore practical steps to cultivating this Christ-like forgiveness within a marriage:

Acknowledge the hurt: The first step is to recognize the pain caused by your spouse's actions. Suppressing your feelings will not make them go away; instead, they will linger and grow, poisoning your heart and hindering your ability to forgive. Allow yourself to feel the hurt and to grieve the betrayal, disappointment, and pain. Don't rush this process; give yourself the time and space needed to process your emotions in a healthy way. Journaling, praying, and talking with a trusted friend or counselor can be helpful during this stage.

Pray for understanding and compassion: Turn to God in prayer, asking for His help in understanding your spouse's perspective and seeing the situation through His eyes. Request that He fills your heart with compassion and empathy, allowing you to view your spouse's actions not as deliberate cruelty but as the result of their own imperfections, struggles, and perhaps even their own pain. Prayer is a powerful tool that can soften the heart and prepare it for forgiveness.

Seek clarity, not judgment: Engage in calm and loving communication with your spouse. Instead of making accusations or placing blame, approach the conversation with a genuine desire to understand their perspective. Ask clarifying questions and listen attentively to their responses. Try to see things from their viewpoint. The goal is not to judge or condemn, but to gain clarity and understand the reasons behind their actions.

Empathize and validate: Even if you don't agree with your spouse's actions, try to understand their motives and the emotions that influenced them. Empathizing with their perspective does not mean condoning their behavior; it means acknowledging their feelings and experiences. Validating their emotions, even if their actions were wrong, demonstrates respect and compassion—crucial steps in the process of forgiveness.

Release the resentment: Holding onto resentment is like carrying a heavy burden. It weighs you down, drains your energy, and prevents you from moving forward. Choose to release that burden and let go of the anger, bitterness, and desire for revenge. While this is not easy, it requires a conscious act of will—a deliberate choice to surrender the control you believe you have over the situation. Instead, embrace the healing power of God.

Practice forgiveness repeatedly: Forgiveness is not a one-time event; it is an ongoing process. There will be times when the pain resurfaces, and the hurt feels as fresh as it did initially. In those moments, you must reaffirm your commitment to forgive, choosing love over resentment and grace over judgment. It is a continuous exercise of your faith and a practice that deepens your relationship with both God and your spouse.

Consider professional help: If you're having difficulty forgiving, consider reaching out for professional help. A mentor, counselor or therapist can offer guidance and support to help you process your emotions and develop healthy coping mechanisms. They can provide strategies for managing difficult conversations and tools to help you move past feelings of unforgiveness.

Remember Christ's example: Reflect upon the life and ministry of Jesus Christ. His life was a living testament to the power of forgiveness. He repeatedly extended grace and mercy to those who wronged him, even to those who crucified him. His forgiveness was not conditional; it was freely given, a demonstration of unconditional love and grace.

Forgiving as Christ forgave is a profound journey, not merely a matter of brushing aside hurt or pretending it never happened. It's a courageous choice to let go of the anger, resentment, and bitterness that can darken our hearts and cloud our relationships with our spouse and God. Imagine choosing love over grudges, healing over hurt, and a future unburdened by the weight of unforgiveness. This act of forgiveness is a beautiful gift—not just to your spouse but to yourself as well. It means aligning your will with God's, reaching for His strength and guidance as you navigate this challenging yet deeply rewarding path.

Now, let's be clear: this process doesn't mean you'll forget the past. Those memories may linger, but true forgiveness transforms their power. Instead of being sources of pain, they can become stepping stones toward growth, empathy, and deeper understanding. It paves the way for healing and rebuilding, giving rise to a relationship that is stronger, more resilient, and filled with love.

Forgiveness acts as a powerful catalyst for spiritual growth. It humbles us, reminding us that we, too, are imperfect and in need of God's grace. It fosters empathy and compassion, deepening our understanding of our partner's struggles. Ultimately, it allows us to experience the incredible transformative power of God's love in our lives, reflecting His boundless mercy in our relationships.

Remember, choosing to forgive is not about minimizing the wrongs done to you; it's about liberating yourself from the pain's grip on your future. It's about taking a step forward, choosing to love fully, and embracing the transformative journey of forgiveness as Christ intended. This choice can reshape your marriage, enhance your relationship with God, and enrich your very being.

It's a journey worth undertaking—a testament to the enduring power of faith, love, and God's unwavering grace. So, embrace this journey! Watch as your marriage flourishes in the fertile ground of forgiveness. The peace that follows will be immeasurable—a reward that far surpasses any pain you've endured.

Of course, the road to forgiveness isn't always smooth. It requires patience, perseverance, and unwavering faith. It's a journey of self-discovery and spiritual awakening, and the process will reshape not only your relationship but also you as individuals. There will be setbacks and moments of doubt when the pain feels almost too much to bear. But always remember, you are never alone. God is right there with you, guiding, strengthening, and providing the grace needed to forgive as Christ did.

Through this transformative process, you will uncover a profound depth of love and resilience within yourselves that you may never have recognized. You will witness the remarkable healing power of God's love, even amid the toughest challenges. Together, you will build a marriage that beautifully reflects the essence of God's infinite mercy and grace.

Loving Your Spouse as Yourself

Exploring the journey of forgiveness in marriage reveals a powerful truth: it's the bedrock for forging a deeper, more meaningful connection with both your spouse and God. But let's take it a step further—creatively intertwining forgiveness with another essential principle: loving your spouse as yourself. This isn't just a heartwarming notion; it's a call to action rooted in scripture and vital for cultivating a fulfilling union.

Imagine love as a vibrant, living force. It's not confined to grand gestures or fleeting romantic moments. Instead, it's about a profound commitment to selflessness, empathy, and mutual respect that shines through in everyday life. Picture prioritizing your spouse's happiness with the same fervor you devote to your own. Acknowledging their worth as beloved children of God transforms your relationship into something truly extraordinary.

Now, loving your spouse as yourself requires a critical self-understanding. Before you can give this kind of love away, you must nurture a healthy appreciation of who you are. Embrace your strengths and weaknesses; recognize your imperfections and forgive yourself for past mishaps. This self-awareness isn't just a feel-good exercise—it's essential. After all, you can't pour from an empty cup; you can only give what you already possess.

Think for a moment about the parable of the Good Samaritan. Here's a figure who stepped outside his comfort zone, displaying selfless love to a stranger in need without any expectation of reward. This is the kind of love we should aspire to replicate in our marriages. It's a love that goes beyond personal convenience—a love that radiates from a place of genuine empathy, willing to sacrifice for the well-being of another.

So, how does this selfless love manifest in our daily lives? It's often found in the little things—the unexpected note tucked into a lunch bag, the patient ear ready to listen without judgment, or the willingness to step in and help during stressful moments. It's about understanding your spouse's perspective, even when it diverges from yours and choosing to uplift rather than criticize. It's giving encouragement instead of finding fault, extending grace where judgment might be easier.

But let's be clear: this doesn't mean ignoring your own needs or sacrificing your well-being. Healthy boundaries are essential! It's all about striking a balance—making a conscious effort to prioritize each other's needs while recognizing how interconnected your lives truly are. Picture that sweet spot where self-care meets selfless love, creating a synergy that elevates both partners and enriches the relationship as a whole.

Consider your marriage a canvas waiting for your brushstrokes. As you embrace forgiveness and selfless love, watch how your relationship transforms into a beautiful work of art, layered with compassion, respect, and an unbreakable bond.

Imagine this: your spouse walks through the door after a long, exhausting day at work. You can see the stress etched on their face. Instead of diving headfirst into your own concerns or complaints, why not take a moment to truly listen? It's in these moments that your love can shine through. You could whip up a comforting meal, offer a soothing massage, or simply sit quietly beside them, letting your presence speak volumes. These small yet meaningful gestures can create a warm atmosphere, showing that you genuinely care.

Now, let's take a step further. What if your spouse mentions a need or desire? Take a moment to assess whether you can help meet that need. It could be something manageable that enriches their day. Stepping up—even if it means putting aside your own plans—can reinforce the bond you share. Remember, it's not about losing yourself; it's about finding harmony where both of you feel valued.

But what if your needs clash? That's when true communication and empathy come into play. Approach the situation with an open mind and a willingness to find common ground. Respectfully share your concerns while genuinely acknowledging your spouse's perspective. This back-and-forth is crucial; it's where compromise becomes a love language. After all, God calls us to love our neighbors as ourselves, and that includes our spouse.

Let's not overlook empathy—it's a powerful tool in love. It's about stepping into your spouse's shoes, understanding their feelings, even if they differ from yours. Picture yourself navigating their situation; this can be a profound way to foster compassion and a deeper connection. Empathy doesn't mean you have to agree; it's about recognizing and validating their feelings.

Respect is another cornerstone of a healthy relationship. It's about cherishing your spouse's thoughts, feelings, and uniqueness, even when they don't align with your own. Treat them with dignity, listen actively, and ensure they feel heard and valued. These actions form a strong foundation for trust and security in your partnership.

And let's talk about acts of service—those little everyday gestures that can make a world of difference. Helping with chores, running errands, or simply being there to lend a hand can express your love and commitment in tangible ways. It doesn't take grand gestures;

often, it's the smallest acts that resonate the most, creating an unbreakable bond between you.

Then there's forgiveness. This isn't always easy, and it's often a repeated act. Choosing love over resentment can be challenging, but it's essential for moving forward together. It's about letting go of anger, continuously extending grace, and making the choice to love again, even when it feels hard.

Ultimately, loving your spouse as yourself reflects a divine love—a beautiful demonstration of selflessness and sacrifice. It's a commitment to put your spouse's needs on par with your own, nurturing a partnership grounded in mutual respect, empathy, and unwavering love. This journey is both an everyday choice and an adventure that transforms not just your marriage but also yourselves. The rewards of this commitment are immeasurable, far outweighing any sacrifices made along the way.

Yes, the path may not always be smooth, but the destination—a love that mirrors the heart of God—makes every step worthwhile. Embrace this journey together, and witness how transformative love can be in your marriage. It's time to create a story worthy of your shared journey, one filled with the richness of God's love woven into every moment.

God's Grace in Marriage

The journey towards a God-centered marriage can feel like an exhilarating adventure, filled with moments of pure joy and times of deep challenge. Picture this: navigating the complexities of human relationships isn't just about making commitments and putting in the work. It calls for a profound reliance on God's grace, which is not a magic wand that erases all difficulties but rather a constant, empowering presence in our lives. This grace is the lifeline that enables us to forgive, to embrace unconditional love, and to persist through the stormiest of seas.

Imagine your marriage as a sturdy ship sailing across a vast, unpredictable ocean. It's built on commitment and effort, strong enough to weather many storms. Yet, even the most resilient vessel will encounter turbulent waters represented by conflicts and challenges that are part of any relationship. The wind may howl, and the waves may crash, threatening to capsize your ship. But what keeps it afloat and on course? God's grace—the unseen hand that gently guides us toward our destination.

This divine grace appears in innumerable forms. It's that quiet whisper of peace amidst heated arguments, the inner strength that compels us to forgive when bitterness threatens to take root, or an unexpected act of kindness that softens a harsh exchange. It's the shared prayer in moments of distress that can mend even the most fractured bonds. Grace allows us to view our spouse not just as a person with flaws, but as a cherished child of God, deserving of our love and compassion, no matter their shortcomings.

Now, let's delve into a more profound challenge: infidelity. Imagine experiencing a wound that feels like a seismic shock to the foundation of your marriage. The instinctive response may be volcanic anger, a sense of betrayal, and a desire for revenge. In the absence of God's grace, it's all too easy to succumb to bitterness, letting resentment fester and threaten to destroy the relationship altogether. Yet, when we lean into God's grace, even this deep wound can begin to heal. It empowers the betrayed spouse to forgive—not because they excuse the betrayal, but because they recognize the transformative power of forgiveness for both hearts involved. It paves the way for compassion, making room for mercy rather than judgment, and while the healing journey may be long and challenging, God's grace lights the path, providing comfort and strength in every step.

Take another scenario: the stress that arises from financial pressures. Money matters can be a significant source of strain, igniting arguments and creating tension where love should flourish. Disagreements over spending habits, budgeting, and priorities can turn couples into adversaries. Those crushing debts can lead to anxiety, pushing partners to the brink. Yet, without God's grace, what could have been a challenge might devolve into accusations and ongoing bickering, eroding mutual respect.

But with God's grace? What a difference it makes! Couples can approach these financial hurdles with a spirit of prayer, humility, and teamwork. They start communicating openly about their finances, developing a budget that reflects their priorities, and learning to distinguish between needs and wants together. Instead of seeing their struggles as mere financial woes, they can transform them into opportunities for faith, growth, and deeper trust in each other and in God's provision.

So, consider this: every trial in our marriage, every storm we face, can also be an invitation to experience God's grace in its truest form. Through prayer, understanding, and unwavering love, our marriages can become a testament to His enduring guidance and mercy.

In the journey of love and marriage, we often encounter a beautiful yet complex tapestry woven from our unique personalities and communication styles. Each of us brings our own perspectives, preferences, and ways of interacting with the world. While these differences can enhance our relationships, they can just as easily spark misunderstandings and conflicts if not handled with care. Without God's grace, such differences could lead to hurtful arguments and a sense of isolation. But with His grace, these same differences transform into opportunities for growth and deeper understanding.

Imagine a couple navigating the ups and downs of life together. With divine grace as their foundation, they learn to see each other's viewpoints as valuable insights rather than points of friction. God's grace empowers them to communicate with empathy, to truly listen, and to find common ground through compromise. This isn't just about finding quick solutions; it's about embracing the journey together, celebrating each other's uniqueness, and building a marriage that thrives on mutual respect and love.

Consider what it means for grace to actively work in their lives. It's not just a passive hope—it's a dynamic force that breathes life into their relationship. It helps them face challenges with courage and resilience, equipping them with the strength to forgive, the willingness to bend, and the capacity to love fiercely, even when the going gets tough.

Think of God's grace as the invisible glue that holds a marriage steadfast against life's storms. It's that divine touch that enables couples to rise above their weaknesses, to communicate openly, and to cultivate a love that mirrors the selfless love of Christ. It serves as a powerful reminder that their union is not merely a product of their efforts, but a sacred covenant blessed by a higher power. When couples embrace this grace, they unlock the potential for a transformative journey—a testament to the unwavering love of God.

Take, for example, a couple grappling with the heart-wrenching challenge of infertility. The longing for children can be an intense and emotional experience, often leading to pain and disappointment. The strain on their relationship may feel overwhelming, with each spouse wrestling with their own grief and frustration. However, when they lean into God's grace, they find a source of strength and solace in their shared faith. Instead of letting the struggle pull them apart, they come together, intertwining their prayers and support, finding comfort in the realization that their worth as individuals and as a couple extends beyond their ability to conceive.

This shared journey through faith may deepen their bond, renewing their commitment to one another. It becomes a powerful reminder of how God's grace sustains them, turning a challenging experience into a profound testament of resilience and love. In these moments, they discover that while the journey may be tough, they do not have to walk it alone—they have each other and, above all, God's unwavering presence guiding them through.

When we think about marriage, it's easy to imagine a love story filled with joy and laughter, but the reality can sometimes include challenging chapters, particularly during tough times like unemployment. Extended periods of joblessness can cast a long shadow over a relationship. The financial strain, coupled with the pressure of supporting a family, can stir up a storm of worries and frustrations. It's in these moments that conversations around spending, budgeting, and priorities can often lead to heated arguments and misunderstandings. The stress of uncertainty can seep into daily life, causing anxiety, tension, and even resentment.

But there's hope! With God's grace, couples can tap into a wellspring of strength that can help them weather these storms. Imagine leaning on your shared faith as a source of support— turning to prayer for solace and encouragement when the road gets rough. Community can play a vital role too, as friends from your faith community can offer not only emotional backing but practical help, reminding you that you're not alone in your struggles. This journey through unemployment, though challenging, can become a powerful testament of resilience. As you navigate these trials together, you uncover a deeper trust in God's plan, strengthening your bond and discovering new depths of love and connection.

Now, let's shift gears to the beautiful yet demanding journey of parenthood. Raising children can feel like a whirlwind, with sleepless nights and an endless to-do list. Parents often find themselves juggling disagreements over parenting styles, discipline tactics, and household chores. It's easy to feel overwhelmed, and left unchecked, these pressures can lead to conflict and a slow fade of intimacy.

Yet, here again, God's grace is the anchor. With grace, couples can learn to communicate openly and respectfully about their differences. Seeking support within your faith community offers a shared space to celebrate victories and navigate the challenges together. Through prayer, you can find clarity and peace amid the chaos, constantly reminded of God's unwavering love that guides you in your parenting journey. This shared experience can catalyze a stronger bond, affirming your commitment to each other as partners in both marriage and parenthood.

Ultimately, embracing God's grace doesn't mean that every day will be free of conflict. Challenges are part of the journey of any human relationship. What grace does offer is a framework—a divine guide for forgiveness, understanding, and growing closer together. Think of it as the fuel that sustains the love and commitment that form the foundation of a God-centered marriage. It's an ongoing adventure, a journey that requires both effort and trust. But the rewards? They're immeasurable. You emerge not only with a closer connection to each other but also a deeper relationship with God.

So, embrace the transformative power of God's grace, and witness firsthand its incredible ability to strengthen, sustain, and ultimately sanctify your union. Your marriage can flourish, growing deeper in love even in the face of life's unexpected challenges. Isn't that a story worth telling?

CHAPTER 7

GROWTH AND TRANSFORMATION IN MARRIAGE

Embarking on a journey of faith together is not just an ordinary experience; it's a beautiful adventure filled with challenges and rewards. As we explore the depths of God's grace, we discover it as the unseen force guiding our marital ship through both calm and stormy waters. But here's the magic: this grace doesn't only strengthen our marriage; it cultivates personal growth in each of us, fortifying the very foundation of our union. Imagine our relationship as two mighty trees, deeply rooted in faith, standing tall side-by-side. As they grow and branch out, their intertwining leaves create a magnificent canopy, symbolizing the strength and beauty of our love. Each tree represents a spouse thriving independently, yet together, they form a resilient forest that can weather any storm.

Personal growth is an exhilarating and ongoing journey of self-discovery and spiritual depth. It calls us to dive deep into our hearts, identify our shortcomings, and aspire to reflect Christ in our daily lives. This journey, though rewarding, can be uncomfortable. It often requires us to face our weaknesses, acknowledge our flaws, and embrace the sometimes-uncomfortable truths about ourselves. Picture it as a process of shedding our old selves, like a caterpillar transforming into a butterfly, stepping into all that God created us to be.

Take pride, for example. It can sneak into our marriages in various forms – the need to always be right, the struggle to admit fault, or the reluctance to compromise. This pride can create distance between us, leeching away the love and understanding we cherish. To dismantle those barriers, we need humility—the courage to own up to our shortcomings and a heartfelt desire to change. Through prayer, honest self-reflection, and seeking wisdom from God's Word, we can replace pride with humility and selflessness, resulting in a marriage that flourishes with love, forgiveness, and compassion.

Forgiveness is another transformative aspect of personal growth. Holding onto resentment can feel like dragging around a heavy anchor, weighing us down and affecting our mood and relationships. But here's the truth: forgiveness is not a sign of weakness; it's the ultimate act of strength. It means releasing the burden of bitterness and choosing love instead. Forgiving our spouse, and ourselves, means confronting the pain head-on, acknowledging the hurt, and making the conscious choice to let go. This can be a powerful journey, nurtured by prayer, wise counsel, and the profound understanding of God's grace, which heals our wounds. When we forgive, we unlock a newfound freedom, paving the way for open communication and deeper connections in our marriage.

Moreover, personal growth shines through when we cultivate self-awareness. Knowing our strengths and weaknesses, as well as our triggers, is essential for navigating the delicate dance of marriage. By becoming more self-aware, we can better manage our reactions in challenging moments, preventing misunderstandings from taking root. It allows us to communicate our needs and desires clearly and respectfully, creating a peaceful and harmonious home. Embracing self-awareness is like holding up a mirror to our spiritual journey, enabling us to identify areas where we need God's intervention and guidance.

The journey of personal growth is like a thrilling adventure—one that invites us to develop healthy coping mechanisms for the inevitable stress and adversity life throws our way. Think of those surprise curveballs: unexpected challenges that test our faith and resilience. How we respond to these trials reveals much about our spiritual maturity.

To navigate life's ups and downs, it's essential to lean on God's strength, seek support from our loved ones, and freely practice self-care. Imagine immersing yourself in activities that spark joy and tranquility—whether it's basking in nature's beauty, diving into hobbies you love, or tapping into your creative side. These habits not only reduce stress but also boost your emotional well-being. When we learn to shoulder our emotional burdens with grace, we can uplift our partners, becoming steady rocks as we face challenges together.

Another vital part of our growth is fostering empathy and compassion. Envision seeing your spouse through God's eyes—discovering their inherent worth and dignity, understanding their struggles and imperfections. It's an essential foundation for nurturing a loving marriage.

Empathy isn't just a buzzword; it's an invitation to step into your spouse's shoes. It's about seeking to grasp their perspectives and feelings, even if you don't always align with them. This compassionate approach doesn't mean endorsing harmful behavior; rather, it encourages us to tackle conflicts with open hearts, striving to build bridges instead of walls. Through prayer, reflection, and intentional efforts, we can deepen our capacity for empathy, enriching the love we share.

The pursuit of spiritual growth also calls us to dive into spiritual disciplines such as prayer, Bible study, and engaging with our community of believers. Think of these practices as nourishment for our souls—they deepen our connection with God and equip us with the tools necessary to tackle life's challenges. Regular prayer can anchor our faith, offer guidance, and strengthen our bond with God. Diving into scripture feeds our minds and hearts with divine wisdom, guiding us toward a life that's truly fulfilling. Being actively involved in a faith community not only fosters support and accountability but also provides a sense of belonging, which is invaluable for our spiritual journeys.

But remember, personal growth is not a solo mission. It's a shared adventure, where we uplift and inspire one another. We can hold each other accountable, celebrate victories together, and extend grace during tough times. When we actively support one another's growth, we create a powerful synergy. Our individual journeys intertwine to fortify our marriage, fostering resilience and fulfillment.

Open communication truly becomes our lifeline; it's vital to express our needs, share our struggles, and celebrate our triumphs with vulnerability and honesty. This collaborative journey cultivates mutual respect, deepens intimacy, and forges a bond so strong it can weather any storm life sends our way.

When we think about personal growth, it's not just a solo endeavor; it's about recognizing our vulnerabilities and finding the courage to seek help when we need it. Let's face it: none of us are perfect. We all stumble, we all face challenges, and it's okay! That's a fundamental part of being human. Reaching out for guidance—whether from wise mentors, professionals, or even extending a heartfelt apology when we've let someone down—isn't a sign of weakness; it's a profound demonstration of maturity and strength.

This willingness to be vulnerable doesn't just enrich our personal journeys; it also deepens the trust and intimacy we share with our spouses. By showing that we are committed to our personal development and our relationship, we build a strong foundation for our marriage.

So, what does it mean to create a God-centered marriage? It's more than just sharing faith or promises; it's about dedicating ourselves to growing spiritually. As each partner strives to draw closer to God—becoming more Christ-like in our thoughts, words, and actions—we not only enhance our own faith but also strengthen the marriage bond itself.

Think of it as a beautiful synergy: personal growth nurtured by God's grace requires conscious effort, self-reflection, and an open heart to embrace change. But trust me, the rewards are absolutely worth it. Imagine a deeper connection with the Divine, fortified individual faith, and a love within your marriage that is vibrant, fulfilling, and enduring.

Just like a thriving forest relies on the strength of each individual tree, your personal growth is essential for the flourishing of your marriage. So, take the time to nurture yourself and watch as your relationship blossoms into a powerful testament to the beauty of God's love. Embrace this journey; it's one that will forever enrich your life and the life of your partner.

Mutual Spiritual Support

The beauty of a God-centered marriage unfolds in profound and unexpected ways, extending beyond shared faith to encompass the rich tapestry of individual growth. Picture this: a vine, intricately entwined with its trellis, stretching upward toward the warmth of the sun. In like manner, we are called to uplift one another on our spiritual journeys. Mutual spiritual support transcends the simple act of attending church together or poring over scripture side by side. It embodies a steadfast commitment to nurturing each other's relationship with God, cheering one another on in pursuing holiness, celebrating victories, finding solace in struggles, and holding each other accountable to the divine purpose etched into our lives.

Imagine two climbers poised to tackle a magnificent mountain together. United by a shared goal—the summit—they embark on unique paths, each facing distinct challenges. One may grapple with a daunting rock face, while the other navigates a slippery ice patch. In those defining moments, mutual support becomes the lifeline. One climber offers a pep talk, a reassuring word, or even a helping hand to pull the other past a grueling section. They exchange stories from their own climbs, sharing wisdom and strength gained from overcoming obstacles. This collaborative journey mirrors the spiritual expedition of a couple; though the path may differ, the shared quest of growing closer to God binds them together.

How does this support manifest? It can be as simple as being a patient listener—truly listening—without judgment as your spouse shares their spiritual highs and lows. It may involve joining in prayer, exchanging words of encouragement, and interceding for one another's needs. It's about inspiring each other to engage in spiritual practices, like daily Bible study or attending a faith community, even on days when motivation wanes. Picture these gentle nudges toward God, celebrating moments of spiritual awakening, and extending grace during times of doubt or struggle.

Consider this scenario: one spouse wrestles with doubt or feels spiritually parched. The other steps in with steadfast support, reminding them of God's unwavering love, sharing comforting scriptures, and praying for renewed strength and faith. This isn't about fixing the issue or dishing out easy answers; rather, it's about being present, offering empathy, and showering unconditional love, allowing room for struggle while affirming their worth, even amidst doubt.

On the flip side, when one spouse uncovers a deep spiritual breakthrough or experiences a season rich in connection with God, the other is there to celebrate that victory, expressing gratitude for the growth and recognizing the blessings that come with it. Such celebrations strengthen their bond, reinforcing their shared commitment to a vibrant faith-filled life. As they share both struggles and triumphs, they deepen their intimacy and strengthen the foundation of their marriage. This creates a haven where vulnerability is embraced, honesty is encouraged, and authenticity is cherished.

But mutual spiritual support does not stop there—it extends to accountability, too. This isn't about judgment or finger-pointing; it's about encouraging and gently nudging each other toward a life that reflects Christ's love and teachings. It may involve highlighting gaps between words and actions, offering constructive feedback, and praying together for the strength to overcome challenges. This kind of accountability isn't punitive; instead, it becomes fertile ground for growth, fostering spiritual maturity and a deeper commitment to following Christ together.

In the journey of marriage, when we cheer, support, and uplift one another, we create a bond that not only honors our commitment to each other but also brings us closer to God—a partnership where love, faith, and growth intertwine beautifully.

Imagine a couple faced with the challenge of one spouse struggling with anger. Instead of becoming frustrated, the other partner steps in with patience and understanding. They listen deeply and suggest healthy coping strategies, such as prayer, meditation, or even seeking counseling together. By joining forces—perhaps praying together or participating in anger management resources—they strengthen their bond and journey toward healing and spiritual growth.

Now, think of the power of serving others together. When couples volunteer at a local soup kitchen or embark on a mission trip, that shared experience can be transformative. It fuses their individual struggles into a collective purpose, fostering empathy and compassion. Rather than being inward-focused, serving directs their energy outward, reinforcing their commitment not just to each other, but to their faith. Each act of kindness becomes a stepping stone, enhancing their relationship and deepening their spiritual connection.

After a fulfilling day of service, envision them reflecting on their experiences. Together, they dive into meaningful conversations about how their actions reflected their beliefs and how they felt God's presence in their service. These moments of shared reflection not only strengthen their bond but also encourage deeper empathy and understanding between them.

Creating a consistent space for spiritual conversations is key. Think of those quiet moments together—whether during prayer time or while on a leisurely walk—where they explore how God is moving in their lives. These conversations don't have to be long theological debates; they can be simple exchanges of thoughts and reflections that foster intimacy and openness.

And when conflict arises, imagine the power of turning to prayer together. Rather than letting disagreements spiral out of control, they seek God's guidance, asking for wisdom and compassion. This shift transforms conflict into an opportunity for growth, reminding them that they are not alone in their challenges. Their marriage, anchored in faith, becomes a vessel for grace and understanding.

It's essential to remember that mutual spiritual support isn't a final destination but an ongoing journey. There will be moments when one partner needs more support, and challenges may test their resilience. But through continual effort, encouragement, and faith, couples can cultivate a profound spiritual partnership that flourishes even amidst life's storms.

The journey of faith shared between them becomes a beautiful testament to the power of mutual spiritual support—a light guiding them toward a deeper, more fulfilling relationship with God and each other. Their individual strengths multiply, creating a marriage that not only withstands difficulties but also shines brightly with God's love, strength, and unyielding commitment. Together, they craft a narrative of resilience, love, and unwavering faith that can inspire those around them.

Overcoming Spiritual Stagnation

Spiritual stagnation—it's that quiet fade, the slow dimming of the vibrant connection you once shared in your marriage. It creeps in, almost unnoticed, leaving behind a feeling of emptiness where faith and fervor used to flourish. Picture this: the once bright flame of your shared spiritual life has dwindled to a flickering ember. But here's the good news—it's not a sign of failure; it's a wake-up call! It's a chance to reignite that passionate fire and deepen your relationship with God, both individually and as a couple.

So, how do you tackle this? Start with some honest self-reflection. Carve out some time—first independently, then together—to truly evaluate your spiritual landscape. Are you engaging in daily devotions, or have they become a forgotten relic? Is your faith community more of an afterthought now? Life's pressures can easily overshadow our spiritual priorities, and it's important to recognize that. Avoid the blame game; instead, focus on those areas where your spiritual connection has lost its spark. Maybe prayer feels routine, Bible study has become a chore, and church feels like just another box to check. Acknowledging these patterns is the first crucial step toward renewal.

Once you've pinpointed the areas that need attention, embrace the power of small, intentional actions. This isn't about making sweeping changes overnight—think gradual, thoughtful re-engagement. Start with bite-sized commitments! Perhaps you could dedicate just one chapter of scripture to read together each morning, followed by a short prayer of thanks or intercession. Or consider diving into a mid-week Bible study or joining a small group focused on spiritual growth. Consistency is key here; even tiny acts of devotion can spark significant change. Imagine it like nurturing a plant: a little bit of water, regularly, can lead to flourishing growth.

Remember, spiritual growth is more like a winding journey than a straight line to an endpoint. There will be days when keeping up with spiritual practices feels heavy or when distractions pull you away. On those tough days, extend grace—to yourselves and to each other. Understand that growth isn't always linear; you might hit plateaus or even feel like you're sliding backward. What matters is that you approach these challenges with humility and a refreshed commitment.

Set aside time for prayer and Bible study together. These shared experiences can weave a stronger spiritual bond between you both. Lift each other up in prayer, confess your shortcomings, and intercede for one another's needs. This mutual vulnerability can deepen intimacy and reinforce your shared faith journey. Think about adopting a consistent prayer routine—whether it's before meals or at bedtime—these moments of togetherness can thread spirituality into the very fabric of your daily life.

Have you ever felt that your spiritual connection with your partner has dimmed a bit? It's a common experience, but the good news is that it's never too late to reignite that spark! Engaging in acts of service together can be a beautiful way to rediscover your spiritual passion. When you pour your energy into helping others, you shift the focus away from personal struggles and anxieties, diving into something much deeper. Whether it's volunteering at a local charity, embarking on a mission trip, or just spreading kindness in your community, these shared experiences can fill your hearts with renewed fulfillment and strengthen your bond as a couple. Remember, each act of service amplifies the shared love and grace of God in your lives!

But don't forget - individual spiritual practices are just as important! Encourage one another on your unique journeys of faith. Maybe one of you finds joy in journaling, while the other thrives in quiet meditation. Celebrate these individual paths! Create a safe space where you can explore and grow separately but still support each other. When one of you has a breakthrough, rejoice together! And during tougher times, offer compassion; this mutual understanding not only solidifies your connection but enriches your shared spiritual life.

Communication is your lifeline when navigating spiritual stagnation. Set aside time to talk openly about your experiences, whether they're uplifting or challenging. Discuss your doubts, fears, and aspirations without judgment. Think of these conversations as your spiritual dialogues; they can lead to profound insights and deepen the intimacy between you. Listening intently and providing empathy are not just nice gestures—they're crucial for sustaining your connection.

Have you considered attending retreats or seminars that focus on spiritual growth and marital enrichment? These events offer the perfect backdrop for meaningful reflection and renewal. Not only will you connect with other couples who share your journey, but you'll also gather practical tools to enhance your relationship with each other and with God. Remember, seeking help from external resources isn't a sign of weakness; it's an intentional step toward growth and deeper understanding.

If you're feeling stuck, don't hesitate to reach out to professionals! A Christian counselor or spiritual director can provide insightful guidance and a safe space for you to navigate challenges together. This isn't about admitting defeat; rather, it's a brave move towards healing and renewal.

Overcoming spiritual stagnation is a journey, not a sprint. It calls for consistent effort, patience, and plenty of grace for each other. Expect moments of doubt and frustration; they are part of the process. But as you engage in spiritual practices, foster open communication, and seek support, you can reignite that spiritual flame. Together, you can deepen your connection with God, building a marriage that beautifully reflects His unwavering love.

As you embark on this journey, remember that you're never alone. God is right there beside you, guiding and supporting every step. Embrace this process, trust in His grace, and let your marriage become a glowing testament to the transformative power of His love. The challenges you face together can lead to immeasurable rewards—a deeply fulfilling and spiritually vibrant marriage awaits.

Continuous Learning and Growth

Embarking on the journey of faith is much like nurturing a meaningful relationship—it requires constant learning and growth. Spiritual maturity isn't a one-time achievement; it's a lifelong adventure of deepening our understanding of God and aligning with

His purpose for our lives. In the realm of marriage, this journey becomes even more profound. Two individuals, each on their unique spiritual path, come together to create a shared life in Christ. It's not about reaching an unattainable ideal of spiritual union but about the daily commitment to seek, strive, and grow together.

So, how can we make this journey exciting and enriching? One of the most impactful ways is through consistent engagement with God's Word. Let's transform reading Scripture from a mundane task into a sacred ritual that deepens our connection with each other and with the divine. Pick passages that speak to your current life stages or dive into various genres of scripture—poetry, prophecy, parables—to unveil the multifaceted character of God. When you discuss the readings, encourage open sharing of interpretations. Don't shy away from healthy disagreements; these respectful conversations can pave the way for deeper insights and spiritual growth for both partners.

But don't stop there! Consider diving into more in-depth Bible studies. This could be a solo journey using study Bibles or engaging in group studies with fellow couples from your church. The shared experience offers support and encouragement that nurtures both individual and collective faith. It's a wonderful way to cultivate accountability, where you can candidly discuss challenges and celebrate each other's victories along the way.

Prayer, too, is an ever-evolving craft that enhances your spiritual partnership. Move beyond the well-worn prayers and explore new forms. Engage in intercessory prayer for each other and the world around you, practice contemplative prayer to draw closer to God, or express spontaneous gratitude and praise. Listening during prayer is crucial—developing a genuine attentiveness to the gentle promptings of the Spirit can lead to richer intimacy and guidance. Consider keeping a joint prayer journal, documenting not just your intentions but also how God responds and the lessons learned throughout the process.

Additionally, don't underestimate the power of wisdom from trusted mentors and spiritual leaders. Seek out a pastor, counselor, or seasoned Christian who can guide you on your journey. Having a safe space to discuss challenges and ask tough questions can be invaluable. Their experiences and insights can provide fresh perspectives and help you navigate the complexities of life together.

And let's not forget the growth opportunities that conferences, workshops, and retreats provide! These events offer exposure to new ideas and practical tools for enhancing both your relationship with God and each other. Embrace these moments to learn and grow, together.

Continuous learning is a dynamic journey, not just a passive intake of information. It's about bringing what we've learned into our daily lives in meaningful ways. As I've mentioned before, you and your spouse decide to step outside your comfort zones and engage in acts of service together. Volunteering at a homeless shelter, visiting the elderly, or supporting a local charity—these experiences not only provide assistance to those in need but also create a powerful bond between you as a couple. As you extend kindness and compassion, you deepen your commitment to serving God, enriching your relationship with a sense of shared purpose that transcends the boundaries of your marriage.

Let's not forget that self-awareness is another critical element of growth. Taking an honest look at your strengths and weaknesses doesn't just illuminate your own journey; it also reveals how these traits impact your relationship with your spouse and God. Make it a habit to reflect regularly—whether through journaling, meditation, or quiet moments of contemplation. This practice allows you to pinpoint areas for improvement and seek divine guidance. Share your spiritual journeys with your partner, discussing both triumphs and struggles without the fear of judgment. This openness nurtures intimacy, creating a safe space for mutual support and understanding.

Don't forget to embrace grace throughout this journey! Spiritual growth isn't a straight path; we all experience moments of doubt, frustration, and setbacks. Recognizing that these challenges are a natural part of the process is key. Show grace to yourselves when things get tough—acknowledge your imperfections and lean into God's unconditional love and forgiveness. Extend that same grace to your spouse, celebrating their strengths and showing compassion during harder times. This cycle of support will not only fortify your connection but also deepen your spiritual ties.

Remember, the ultimate goal isn't perfection; it's progress. It's not about hitting a flawless mark of spiritual maturity, but continually striving to embody the love of Christ, both individually and as a couple. This ongoing journey of learning and growth will strengthen your marriage, enriching your love and connection with God. So, embrace the challenges, celebrate the victories, and trust in God's unwavering love to guide you along this beautiful, lifelong adventure. The rewards of pursuing spiritual maturity together far outweigh any difficulties. Let your marriage stand as a vibrant testament to the transformative power of God's love.

Spiritual Renewal and Recommitment

The journey of spiritual growth is not one we embark on alone; it's a beautiful pilgrimage shared with our spouse. Just like a garden flourishes with regular care, the spiritual landscape of our marriage requires nurturing too. This means setting aside time for intentional spiritual renewal and recommitment, moments that go beyond mere maintenance to foster vibrant flourishing. These are not just times for quiet reflection but active choices to rededicate ourselves to God and to the sacred vows we've shared.

One of the most enriching paths to spiritual renewal is through intentional retreats. Don't worry; these retreats don't have to be extravagant, week-long getaways. They can be simple yet profound—a weekend escape, a peaceful day in nature, or even just a few hours spent in heartfelt prayer in a cozy corner of your home. The essence lies in creating a sanctuary devoid of distractions, a space where you can unplug from life's chaos and reconnect with each other and your faith. Picture a snug cabin tucked away in the woods, where the soft crackling of a fire accompanies whispered prayers and intimate conversations. Or imagine the serenity of a quiet beach, where the gentle rhythm of waves washes away your worries, allowing you to share your dreams and hopes for the future. These moments, however fleeting, enable deep introspection and breathe new life into your shared purpose.

During these retreats, engaging in practices like silent reflection or contemplative prayer can yield profound transformations. Silent reflection provides an opportunity to drown out the mental noise and attune your ears to the subtle whispers of the Spirit. It's not about emptying your mind completely but making space for God's voice to rise amid daily distractions. Contemplative prayer, often characterized by the repetition of a single word or phrase, can deepen your communion with God, instilling a sense of peace and tranquility. Visualize the calm settling over you as you gently repeat a phrase, such as "Abba Father," (Romans 8:15-16) letting it wash over you, soothing your spirit and bringing your focus back to the divine.

Reaffirming your marriage vows can also serve as a powerful catalyst for spiritual renewal. This isn't mere recitation; it's a deliberate act of recommitment, a heartfelt reaffirmation of the promises made before God and loved ones. This moment should transcend the ordinary—reflect on the journey you've traveled together, celebrating both the joys and the challenges, the triumphs and setbacks. To make it even more special, consider crafting new vows that resonate with your growth and evolving understanding of your commitment. Let them reflect your renewed dedication to one another within the context of your deepened faith.

Imagine a moment where the hustle and bustle of life fades away, and you find yourselves once again enveloped in each other's warmth. This reaffirmation of your love can take many beautiful forms. Picture a cozy, intimate ceremony in the comfort of your home, just the two of you. Candles flicker softly, and gentle music fills the air, creating a sacred atmosphere where your hearts can truly connect. Alternatively, envision a grander renewal of vows at your church, surrounded by beloved family and friends—an uplifting celebration of your enduring love and unwavering faithfulness. Regardless of how you choose to express it, the essence remains unchanged: a heartfelt recommitment to your marriage and your shared spiritual journey. As you exchange vows, let the weight of your promises sink in, feeling the power of your commitment rooted deeply in faith and love.

But don't stop there! Beyond those moments of formal reaffirmation, there are countless ways to infuse your daily lives with spiritual renewal. How about establishing a weekly ritual of shared prayer and Bible study? It can be as simple as curling up together with a meaningful passage, discussing its implications, and lifting each other up in prayer. This consistency creates a delightful rhythm in your spiritual life, a comforting oasis amidst the challenges of daily living.

Now, let's take it a step further! Imagine the joy of volunteering together at a local charity, visiting the elderly, or even just helping a neighbor in need. These acts of service are a tangible expression of your faith, providing you with an opportunity to deepen your connection with each other as you work side by side. Feel the shared purpose and the warmth of compassion fueling your actions, allowing you to serve God while simultaneously enriching your relationship. The joy of giving not only uplifts those you help but also infuses your bond with unity and purpose, creating lasting memories together.

Another key element of this spiritual renewal journey is open, honest communication about your individual spiritual paths. This doesn't mean diving into deep theological debates; instead, it's about sharing your personal experiences of faith—your struggles, triumphs, doubts, and moments of clarity. By opening up to one another, you create a sanctuary of vulnerability, where trust flourishes and mutual support becomes second nature. Picture the relief and closeness as you share your true selves, cultivating an environment of authenticity and transparency.

Remember, spiritual renewal isn't just about mending what's broken; it's about nurturing and strengthening the beauty that already exists. Think of it as tending to the garden of your marriage, ensuring its roots grow deep and its flowers bloom vibrantly. It takes intentional time and effort, but the rewards are beyond measure. As you deepen your faith and strengthen your connection, you'll witness a blossoming of love that reflects the transformative power of spiritual renewal.

In any marriage, the journey of love is both beautiful and complex, filled with opportunities for growth and connection. One of the most powerful tools we have at our disposal is the practice of regular confession and forgiveness. Let's face it—we're all imperfect. Disagreements and misunderstandings are bound to happen. By openly acknowledging our shortcomings, both to God and to each other, we can lift the weight of guilt and resentment off our hearts. This act of confession isn't just about admitting our faults; it's about creating space for healing and rebuilding trust.

133

When we forgive, we take a brave step beyond our past pains, igniting a cycle of grace and compassion that strengthens our bond.

But let's not stop there! Think about adding a splash of creativity to your spiritual renewal. How about turning up some uplifting music and singing hymns together? Or writing poetry and songs that reflect your faith journey? You can get crafty by engaging in artistic projects that symbolize your spiritual connection. These creative avenues not only express love for God but also cultivate a shared experience that deepens your intimacy. Imagine the joy in creating something beautiful together that resonates with your hearts!

As you embark on this journey of spiritual renewal, remember—it's not a race to a finish line but a lifelong adventure. There will be bumps in the road and moments of doubt, but it's precisely through these challenges that your faith is sharpened and your love deepened. Embrace this journey wholeheartedly, with patience, perseverance, and a grateful spirit. You might just find that the depth of your intimacy and spiritual connection becomes something you never imagined possible.

In time, your marriage can stand as a testament to the transformative power of God's love. It can shine as a beacon of hope and inspiration for others navigating their paths. The effort you put into nurturing your spiritual journeys together will far outweigh any obstacles you face. You are co-authors of a love story that not only reflects your unique bond but also the incredible essence of God's grace.

CHAPTER 8

LEAVING A LEGACY OF FAITH

Our journey of faith is not just about our spiritual growth; it's deeply connected to the legacy we establish, especially in the lives of our children. Raising godly children isn't a passive task; it requires intentionality, consistent modeling, and unwavering commitment. Think of it as cultivating a beautiful garden—a place where seeds of faith are sown with care, nurtured with love, and watered with prayer, ultimately blossoming into something vibrant, reflecting God's grace.

At the core of raising godly children is our own foundation. Kids are sharp observers; they mirror our actions more than they listen to our words. They don't just learn from moral lectures; they absorb the practical application of our faith in everyday life. If we emphasize honesty but slip into white lies or convenient omissions, our children will likely follow suit. If we proclaim compassion yet show impatience towards others, they will see those actions as acceptable. Therefore, it's crucial to embody the principles of Christ—showing love, forgiveness, humility, and integrity. It's not just about teaching them faith; it's about living it.

This doesn't mean we need to be perfect; in fact, it's quite the opposite. Children learn from our missteps just as much, if not more, than they do from our successes. When we make mistakes—something we all do—it creates an invaluable teaching moment. Acknowledging our flaws, seeking forgiveness from God and those we've hurt, and demonstrating true repentance offers powerful lessons in humility and the transformative power of grace. Showing our authentic selves, with all our imperfections, is far more impactful than pretending to be flawless. It teaches them that faith isn't about reaching an unattainable ideal but about striving for holiness amid our human flaws. This message resonates deep within the human heart—it's a testament to the enduring power of God's grace, filled with hope and redemption.

Incorporating prayer into our family life is more than just a good practice—it's a game changer. Think about it: family prayer at mealtime, bedtime, or whenever it fits into our busy schedules creates a sacred moment where we all come together to connect with God. It's about more than reciting phrases; it's a heartfelt chat with our Creator! We express our gratitude, ask for guidance, and acknowledge how much we truly depend on Him. When our children observe this, they learn that prayer isn't a performance but a genuine bond with God. It becomes an integral part of their daily lives, gently shaping how they see the world and understand their faith.

Similarly, diving into the Bible can be a thrilling adventure! It's not just about reading the scriptures; it's about engaging with them—letting the stories challenge us, inspire us, and transform our hearts. Family Bible study is a unique way to foster a love for God's Word in our kids. Rather than just memorizing verses, we can explore the rich narratives, parables, and teachings together. Imagine interactive discussions, creative activities, or even dramatizing

Bible stories. This approach makes the Bible feel alive and relevant, breathing fresh meaning into its ancient texts!

On top of that, embracing religious education and mentorship is essential. Sunday school, youth groups, and faith communities open up incredible pathways for our children to connect with peers who are walking the same faith journey. These interactions foster a sense of belonging, while mentors—those remarkable individuals who embody godly character—provide invaluable support and guidance. Think of them as supportive branches that nurture the trunk of our family faith, enriching the growth of our children and broadening their spiritual perspectives.

Now, let's talk about discipline. It's a crucial element of raising children who reflect godly values, but it should always come from a place of love and kindness. Instead of viewing discipline as punishment, we can approach it as an opportunity to teach, guide, and correct. Setting boundaries teaches our children about responsibility and self-control, but we must do it with compassion, rooted in God's love. The goal? To shape their character through gentle guidance—not fear.

Alongside this, fostering a spirit of service and compassion is incredibly important. Volunteering at a local charity or participating in community acts of kindness are fantastic ways to live out our faith practically. These experiences aren't just charitable but also powerful opportunities to model Christian values, teaching our children about empathy and responsibility. By seeing faith in action, they understand that living in faith means being active and engaged in serving others.

Open communication and honesty are vital throughout this journey. It's essential to create a safe space where our children feel comfortable discussing their faith, doubts, and struggles. When we listen actively without judgment, we show them that their questions and concerns matter. This fosters trust and encourages an open dialogue, ensuring they know they can approach us with anything—knowing they'll receive guidance and understanding, not condemnation.

Finally, let's remember that raising godly children is a marathon, not a sprint. It's a lifelong journey filled with nurturing, guidance, and support. There will be challenges, doubts, and uncertainties, but it's through these trials that we and our children deepen our faith. This journey is all about love, grace, and continual growth—one that leaves an enduring legacy for generations. The rewards of this path are immeasurable and far outweigh any momentary struggles. The legacy you build, grounded in faith and love, will blossom beyond your lifetime. The seeds you plant today will grow into a beautiful testament to God's grace, creating a legacy of faith that impacts lives for years to come.

Mentoring Younger Couples

Our journey of faith isn't just about us; it's about reaching out and helping others, especially younger couples trying to figure out the whole marriage and faith thing. Mentoring them can be such a meaningful thing! It's not just a nice gesture; it's a way to leave a legacy of faith that can impact generations to come.

Think about it like passing the torch. We've all been there, facing our own ups and downs, learning from our mistakes, and celebrating our victories. By sharing our experiences, we can help younger couples avoid some of the stumbling blocks we hit and encourage them to grow spiritually.

When we're mentoring, it's not about telling them what to do or forcing our beliefs on them. It's more about walking alongside them—offering support and a listening ear. We want to create a safe space where they can be open about their struggles without fear of judgment and get advice that's rooted in love and faith. Sometimes, the best thing we can do is just listen!

One of the best ways to support younger couples is through prayer. Imagine lifting their challenges up to God—that's powerful! Praying with them encourages a sense of community and helps them see how they can bring their joys and struggles to God. It's not just about asking for blessings; it's about seeking wisdom for the specific issues they're dealing with. Sharing prayer can really deepen their spiritual connection and strengthen their relationship.

But let's not just stop at prayer. Sharing our faith journey is huge, too! We don't want to come off as bragging about our perfect lives; instead, it's important to be real about our struggles and how we've learned from them. Young couples need to know that faith is less about being perfect and more about growing and relying on God through the good and bad times. If we can share our experiences— like how we handled conflicts, challenges with kids, or financial stress—those stories can be really encouraging and helpful for them.

And don't forget about practical tips! If we've found books, articles, or workshops that helped us in our marriages, why not share them? We could suggest fun ideas like date nights that focus on prayer or discussion, or even reading scripture together regularly. Those practical suggestions, tailored to what each couple needs, can really make a difference. Ultimately, mentoring isn't just about passing down what we know; it's about walking alongside the next generation, supporting them, and creating a legacy of faith and love that lasts.

Mentoring also involves providing opportunities for spiritual growth. We can invite younger couples to join us in activities that foster spiritual development, such as Bible studies, retreats, or community service projects. These shared experiences can enrich their faith and strengthen their bonds with other believers, offering a support system outside their immediate relationship. Participating in community service together can also model the importance of serving others and living out one's faith in tangible ways. The shared experience fosters a deeper understanding of Christian values and strengthens their commitment to living a life that honors God.

Open communication is essential in mentorship. Creating a safe space where younger couples feel comfortable sharing their vulnerabilities, their doubts, and their fears is paramount. We need to listen actively, without judgment, offering empathy and understanding, even when their perspectives differ from our own. It's important to remember that our role isn't to judge or criticize, but to guide and support. This open communication fosters trust, allowing them to approach us with any challenges they face, knowing they'll receive guidance rooted in compassion and understanding. It's about creating a space for honest conversations, encouraging vulnerability, and providing a safe place to express doubts and fears.

We must also remember that mentorship is a two-way street. As we mentor younger couples, we also learn from them. Their perspectives, their challenges, and their growth can offer valuable insights and remind us of the enduring power of faith. It's a mutual exchange of wisdom, experience, and support, enriching our own spiritual lives and strengthening our faith.

Finally, we need to remember that mentoring is a long-term commitment. It's not a one-time event, but a continuous process of support, guidance, and encouragement. It requires patience, understanding, and unwavering commitment. There will be times when we may feel frustrated or discouraged, but we must persevere, trusting that God will use our efforts to strengthen younger couples and leave a lasting legacy of faith. The investment of time and energy we dedicate to mentoring others is a tangible expression of our faith, demonstrating the importance of investing in others' spiritual growth.

The rewards of mentoring younger couples are immeasurable. We not only strengthen their marriages and their faith, but we also enrich our own lives, deepening our relationship with God and leaving a legacy that extends far beyond our own lifetimes. It's a powerful act of love, a testament to our commitment to passing on the torch of faith, ensuring that the flame burns brightly for generations to come. It is a commitment to the ongoing work of God's kingdom, ensuring the flourishing of faith in the hearts of others. The impact we have is far-reaching, influencing not only the couples we mentor but also the families they build, and the communities they serve. It's a profound act of service, a ripple effect of faith that continues to expand, a testament to the enduring power of God's grace. This legacy of faith, cultivated through mentorship and nurtured through prayer and shared experiences, is a gift beyond measure, a treasure that will continue to grow and flourish long after we are gone.

Leaving a Lasting Spiritual Impact

Our journey of faith doesn't end with just nurturing younger couples; it's a vibrant tapestry that weaves through our entire community and the world at large. This isn't about striving for grand, public accolades or showcasing piety; rather, it's about infusing faith into the everyday moments of our lives. Picture it: acts of service, generosity, and profound compassion become our way of life, reflecting the love and grace of God in ways that quietly yet powerfully touch those around us.

One of the most impactful ways we can leave a lasting spiritual footprint is through consistent acts of service. This isn't about fleeting moments of charity; it's about embedding service deep within our hearts. Imagine seeing the needs of others not as burdens but as golden opportunities to express God's love. It could be volunteering at a local soup kitchen, mentoring underprivileged children, or bringing joy to the sick in hospitals and nursing homes. Even something as simple as offering a helping hand to a neighbor can be transformative. The value lies not only in the action itself but also in the spirit behind it—serving with humility while recognizing our own imperfections and leaning on God's grace to guide our way.

Consider again the parable of the Good Samaritan. He didn't think twice about helping a stranger, regardless of their background or situation. His actions broke societal norms, showcasing the boundless love of God. We, too, can embody this spirit of compassion, reaching out to those on the edges of society, the ones often overlooked or ignored. It's about recognizing Christ within each person, discovering the divine spark in every encounter, no matter their beliefs or actions. When we do this, our seemingly simple acts of service blossom into profound expressions of faith.

Generosity, in all its forms, is another essential element of leaving that lasting spiritual impact. It goes beyond monetary contributions—though, yes, giving is important. It's about a heart that's open and willing to share; it's about offering our time, our skills, our resources, and our love. Imagine looking at what we have not as possessions to cling to but as blessings we're meant to share with those in need.

Think of the widow who contributed her two mites—a seemingly insignificant amount. Yet, her offering shone brightly, celebrated for its selfless devotion. It wasn't about how much she gave but the spirit of sacrifice and gratitude that fueled her gift. This serves as a reminder that true generosity flows from a heart that's brimming with thankfulness for God's blessings.

But generosity doesn't stop at material things. We can pour ourselves into others by sharing our knowledge, skills, experiences, and time. Mentoring, as we've seen, is a profound act of generosity. By investing in the lives of others, we help them flourish in their faith journeys. Sharing our own stories—our struggles, victories, and lessons learned—can inspire and uplift others as they navigate their spiritual paths. This act of vulnerability not only fosters connection but also builds community, creating a space where we support one another in faith. After all, faith isn't a solitary endeavor; it's a shared journey, illuminated by the love and grace of God.

Compassion lies at the heart of the Christian faith—it's that deep, heartfelt ability to truly feel for those who are suffering. Imagine a world where we all took the time to acknowledge the pain and struggles of others, extending a hand of comfort and understanding without an ounce of judgment. This is the essence of compassion: mirroring the unconditional love of Christ, we learn to offer grace even to those who may have wronged us. It's a transformative journey that requires us to shift from our own self-centeredness to a genuine concern for the well-being of those around us.

Picture this: sitting down with someone who has just shared their story of hardship. You listen intently, your heart open, validating their experiences and providing a shoulder to lean on. This kind of presence—physically, emotionally, and spiritually—creates a sanctuary of peace and understanding for those in need.

But let's take it a step further! Leaving a lasting spiritual impact isn't just about individual acts of kindness; it's about weaving together strong, vibrant faith communities. These communities become safe havens—offering support, encouragement, and opportunities for spiritual growth. When we gather in prayer, worship, and fellowship, we create a network of believers who uplift one another, helping us all navigate through life's challenges. By participating actively in these communities, we are not just enhancing our own spiritual journeys; we're collectively illuminating God's purpose.

And let's not forget about our interactions beyond our immediate circles. Imagine demonstrating Christian values—love, forgiveness, patience, kindness—in every encounter, no matter how seemingly small. By embodying the teachings of Christ in our daily lives, we become living examples of His love and grace. Engaging in respectful dialogue with others who hold different beliefs, while listening with humility, can create powerful connections. Recognizing the inherent dignity in every person, regardless of background or faith, showcases the true nature of empathy and can have a profound influence.

Fostering forgiveness is another critical element in our spiritual journey. Holding on to resentment only drags us down, but letting go is liberating! Embracing forgiveness allows us to free ourselves from past burdens and experience the peace that comes from God's grace. This act paves the way for positive relationships, harmony, and understanding within our families and communities.

Leaving a lasting spiritual impact is not simply a goal; it's a lifelong journey filled with growth, learning, and transformation. It's about continually striving to reflect the love, grace, and compassion of Christ in our thoughts, words, and actions. Picture yourself seeking God's guidance, relying on His strength, and trusting in His divine plan. Each thoughtful action creates ripples that extend far beyond our lives, impacting generations to come.

Ultimately, what defines our legacy is not what we accomplish or possess, but how we touch the lives of others. The love we share is a gift to the world, a powerful testament to the transformative nature of God's grace. This legacy, grounded in a life of faithful service, serves as a beacon of hope for future generations.

As we embrace this ongoing dedication to our faith and the pursuit of love and grace, we create an enduring legacy—one that continues to inspire and uplift long after we're gone. Together, let's cultivate that enduring spirit, lighting the path for others to follow, and making this world a more compassionate place.

Sharing Your Story

Sharing our journey—complete with triumphs and stumbles— might just be one of the most powerful legacies we can leave behind. It serves as a testament to the transformative power of faith, acting as a beacon of hope that illuminates the path for others walking similar roads. Many couples hold back, fearing vulnerability or judgment, but it's precisely in that vulnerability where genuine connection and inspiration thrive.

Our story isn't meant to be a flawless narrative of a perfect marriage. Instead, it's a testament to the enduring power of faith amidst adversity—a vivid demonstration of how God's grace can mend brokenness and strengthen bonds.

What makes sharing our story beautiful is its authenticity. It's about being honest about our struggles, doubts, and moments of sheer despair, recognizing that faith isn't a protective shield against hardship but rather a compass guiding us through life's storms. We've faced challenges—discord, misunderstandings, and times when our faith felt fragile. Instead of hiding those moments, we can view them as opportunities to share the raw reality of our faith journey. Even during turmoil, God's love remains steadfast. By laying bare these vulnerable moments, we create a space for others to feel seen, heard, and understood in their own challenges. We remind them that they aren't alone in their imperfections, and that God's grace is sufficient for every trial.

Sharing our story isn't about self-promotion; it's about offering hope and encouragement to those navigating their own spiritual journeys. It's about showing that faith is a lived experience—a daily walk with God filled with joy and sorrow, triumph and tribulation. In our shared experiences, we offer others a tangible example of how faith can sustain them during life's most challenging moments. We provide a glimpse into a faith-filled marriage, revealing how a deep connection with God can strengthen and enrich marital bonds.

You might wonder, how do we effectively share our story? Truthfully, there's no one-size-fits-all method, but rather a multitude of avenues, each uniquely suited to different contexts and audiences. One powerful approach is through personal conversations. Sharing snippets of our journey with friends, family, or members of our church community can foster meaningful connections and create a supportive network of fellow travelers on their faith journeys. Those informal chats allow for organic exchanges about struggles and triumphs, weaving faith seamlessly into our conversations.

Another impactful way to share our story is through written testimonials. Whether it's a brief reflection in a church newsletter or a longer narrative in a faith-based magazine or blog, written accounts offer us the space for thoughtful reflection. They allow us to articulate key themes and experiences while carefully crafting our message. It's vital, however, to maintain a spirit of humility in these accounts—focusing on God's grace and the lessons learned rather than personal achievements.

In our journey of faith, we've discovered that small group discussions within our church can be incredibly transformative. These intimate gatherings provide a safe space where we can share our stories and be vulnerable with one another. There's something powerful about sitting in a circle, exchanging thoughts and experiences, that cultivates an atmosphere of mutual support and encouragement. It's in these moments that we realize we are not alone; we are part of a community of fellow travelers navigating similar challenges. The spontaneous conversations that arise in these discussions can clarify misunderstandings and tackle specific questions we may have, making the experience feel more genuine and connected than any formal presentation could.

On the other hand, public speaking can be a bit intimidating for some, but it offers a chance to reach a wider audience with our testimony. With careful planning and a little creativity, we can craft well-structured presentations filled with personal anecdotes that resonate deeply with others. The trick lies in being authentic— sharing our experiences with empathy, encouraging self-reflection, and avoiding a preachy tone. When done right, a thoughtfully prepared talk can light a fire in the hearts of many and inspire them to embark on their own spiritual journeys.

But let's not forget, our daily lives are brimming with opportunities to share our faith in meaningful and subtle ways. The way we conduct ourselves—through our words, actions, and attitudes— serves as a quiet yet powerful testament to our commitment to God. Simple acts of kindness and compassion can speak volumes, showcasing God's love in action and illustrating the profound impact of faith without the need for grand speeches.

Even within the ebb and flow of our daily routines, we encounter countless opportunities to weave our faith into the fabric of our lives. Whether it's sharing a challenge we've overcome, offering a prayer for a friend in need, or volunteering our time to serve the community, these small yet significant actions have immense spiritual weight. They're reminders that our faith is alive and vibrant, influencing our interactions with others in profound ways.

Sharing our story isn't just a one-time event but an ongoing journey of reflection and connection. It's about being willing to show up, be vulnerable, and articulate our experiences in an authentic way. The rewards of this journey are immeasurable. When we share our stories, we create ripples of hope, inspiring others to embrace their own faith journeys. We strengthen our community bonds and leave a legacy of faith that reverberates through time.

Remember, our stories aren't about being perfect; they're about progress. Each of us has a journey marked by triumphs and setbacks, doubt and unwavering belief. When we share these raw, unfiltered moments, we open the door for others to relate, find solace, and feel less isolated in their struggles. We show that faith isn't about perfection; it's about wrestling with the messy realities of life and finding growth in the process.

The act of sharing goes beyond mere storytelling; it becomes an act of ministry and an offering of hope. It's a profound act of love that extends grace and compassion to those feeling lost on their own paths. By sharing our experiences, we fulfill the Great Commission, spreading the message of God's love through our journeys, vulnerabilities, and enduring faith. Each story we share contributes to a beautiful tapestry of faith, intertwining our individual threads into a grand narrative of God's grace.

In this sharing lies the power to inspire others to embark on their journeys of faith, love, and service. Our imperfect stories become beacons of hope, leaving a legacy that impacts generations to come. So, let's embrace the wonderful opportunity we have to share our stories, knowing that in doing so, we reflect the transformative power of God's love.

Creating a Family Tradition of Faith

Building a strong foundation of faith within your family is about so much more than just attending church services or reciting prayers. It's about creating a vibrant tapestry of beliefs that enriches everyday life together. Think of it as crafting family traditions that nurture spiritual growth, connect hearts, and create lasting memories that weave generations together. These traditions are living expressions of faith—flexible and unique to your family's personality and dynamics. In the face of life's ups and downs, they serve as anchors, offering stability, comfort, and a shared sense of purpose.

One of the most impactful ways to nurture a family tradition of faith is through regular family devotions. You don't need to plan elaborate rituals or lengthy sessions. Just a simple five-minute prayer time before dinner, where each family member shares a prayer request or a word of gratitude, can create profound connections. Reading a Bible passage together and discussing its meaning can lead to engaging conversations and a deeper understanding of scripture. Children particularly benefit from hearing scripture read aloud—it's a wonderful way to make faith engaging and accessible. These shared moments cultivate family unity and a sense of shared purpose, proving that it's the consistency of these devotions that truly matters, not their length or complexity.

As you embark on this devotional journey, remember to tailor your focus to your children's ages and interests. For younger kids, vibrant storybooks featuring biblical heroes or age-appropriate Bible videos can ignite their curiosity. For older children, diving into deeper discussions about moral dilemmas or how to apply biblical teachings to everyday life can be incredibly rewarding. Encourage creativity with interactive activities, like drawing scenes from the stories or writing personal reflections. The goal? To inspire a love for God's word and a heartfelt desire to understand His teachings—not to impose strict dogma.

But faith doesn't have to be confined to devotions; it can seamlessly blend into family fun time, too! Imagine a family game night centered around faith-based games that inspire teamwork and reinforce spiritual values. Or consider volunteering together at a local homeless shelter or food bank—these experiences cultivate compassion and empathy while vividly demonstrating faith in action. The memories you create during these shared experiences will become cherished moments that bind your family closer together.

While regular church attendance is a cornerstone for many faith-driven families, it's essential to actively participate in church life. Joining a small group, volunteering for events, or being part of the choir can deepen your sense of belonging and engagement. These experiences not only connect you with others who share your faith but also foster mutual support and encouragement within your family.

Celebrate religious holidays with intention. Instead of simply focusing on gifts or food, engage in meaningful reflections, read relevant Bible passages, and practice charitable giving. Consider creating unique traditions, such as making ornaments for the Christmas tree as a family or incorporating themes of resurrection into your Easter egg hunts. These practices turn special occasions into opportunities for spiritual growth and family bonding, celebrating God's love and the heart of your faith.

Another enriching tradition to consider is making prayer walks a regular part of your family life. Take leisurely strolls in nature together, soaking in the beauty of God's creation as you pray. This relaxed atmosphere encourages open communication and heartfelt discussions, fostering deeper connections among family members.

Plus, these shared experiences in the outdoors not only create lasting memories but also strengthen the bonds that tie your family together.

Incorporating acts of kindness into your family's routine can be a transformative and heartwarming experience. Imagine your family regularly volunteering at a local charity or helping an elderly neighbor; these little gestures resonate deeply with the love and compassion that Christ exemplified. Not only do these acts of service create opportunities for teamwork, but they also teach children the value of empathy and caring for others, reinforcing the core principles of faith within your family.

Consider how these shared experiences can strengthen your family bond while also making a positive impact in the community around you. From donating blood to lending a hand with yard work, the options for kindness are endless. Remember that family traditions aren't set in stone; they can grow and adapt just like your family does. What worked well when your children were young may not be the best fit for teenagers. Keeping the essence of love and faith at the forefront, you can adjust your family traditions to remain relevant and engaging at every stage of life.

The real power lies not only in these activities but in the memories created together—the laughter, reflection, and moments of growth that weave a rich tapestry of faith. These traditions serve as a constant reminder of the unwavering love and commitment that binds your family. By creating a space where faith intertwines with everyday life, you nurture a loving environment that can inspire generations to come.

Why not spice things up with some journaling? Each family member can maintain a personal journal filled with reflections, prayers, and spiritual insights. This practice not only encourages personal growth but also deepens understanding of one another's spiritual journeys. Sharing snippets from these journals during family devotions can foster connection and vulnerability, building a stronger understanding of each other's relationships with God.

You could also try creating a family "faith tree" or a visual representation of your spiritual growth. Each member can add leaves or ornaments to symbolize significant events, blessings, or lessons learned along the way. This visual testament will serve as a beautiful reminder of God's presence in your family's life, showcasing your shared experiences and united growth on your spiritual journey.

Creating family traditions is an exciting journey, not a fixed destination. It's perfectly natural for traditions to evolve or even fade away as life changes—what matters is that the core values of love, faith, and family unity remain central to your family's story. Embracing flexibility and adaptability will allow these traditions to thrive and nurture a strong, faith-filled family environment.

Ultimately, the objective is to raise children who are firmly grounded in their faith, ready to tackle life's challenges, and motivated to share their beliefs with others. This isn't just about your immediate family; it's about cultivating a legacy of faith that echoes beyond your home, impacting communities and the world. Think of it as a gift that keeps on giving—shaping not only the lives of your children but also the lives of future generations. By consistently making these intentional efforts, your family can build a rich legacy of faith that strengthens your bond and leaves a lasting mark on the world. So, why not embark on this beautiful journey together? It's an adventure that promises growth, joy, and a deeper connection to each other and to faith.

CHAPTER 9

A LASTING COVENANT

Commitment. Just saying the word evokes a sense of strength and steadfastness, reflecting the boundless nature of God's love. It's a term we often bandy about, yet its true depth is frequently overlooked, especially in the sacred bond of marriage. Commitment is not just a feeling or a momentary emotion; it's an unwavering choice we make daily—to stand by our partner through life's storms and sunshine, triumphs and tribulations. In a world that promotes fleeting passions and disposable relationships, the enduring power of commitment stands as a beacon of hope, showcasing faith's transformative ability.

This kind of commitment, grounded in faith, demands more than passive acceptance of challenges; it calls for active engagement in nurturing a relationship that mirrors God's unwavering love for us. It invites us to confront our own imperfections and view conflict not as an enemy but as an opportunity for growth and understanding. Humility is key here—it's about letting go of ego and embracing a higher calling of love. This journey requires a profound understanding of forgiveness; it's about extending grace to our spouse while also allowing grace for ourselves. We are human—flawed and broken—constantly in need of God's mercy and each other's understanding.

Consider the parable of the vineyard: the owner plants, nurtures, and tends his vines, even amidst weeds and harsh conditions. His unwavering commitment reflects our own dedication to our spouses. We invest time, energy, and love, knowing the resulting harvest may not be immediate but will be deeply rewarding in the long run. Even when faced with thorny challenges, we continue watering the vines, weeding out negativity, and trusting the divine process guiding our growth.

This enduring commitment is crucial when life throws unexpected challenges our way. Life isn't a fairytale; it's a journey filled with unpredictable turns. We'll experience seasons of drought alongside abundant times, overwhelming joy mingled with profound sorrow. Our commitment acts as an anchor during these turbulent times, providing stability and emotional refuge amidst adversity. It isn't conditioned on happiness; rather, it remains steadfast, revealing its true strength during hardships.

Moreover, commitment in marriage transcends personal bonds—it's a reflection of our commitment to God. It's a public declaration of our faith, symbolizing the powerful love that flows through our lives. Our marriage is a living testament to the sacred union between Christ and His church. Thus, our commitment encompasses nurturing this sacred bond and upholding its sanctity in all we do. This means engaging in prayer, seeking wise counsel, and continually striving to honor our vows—both to God and to one another.

Look at couples who have embraced decades of marriage, weathering storms that could shatter less resilient bonds. Their enduring love isn't simple luck; it's a testament to their unwavering commitment to nurture their relationship through thick and thin.

They've learned to forgive, compromise, and communicate openly, investing not just emotionally but spiritually in their connection. By praying together and creating traditions that strengthen their bond, they demonstrate that commitment isn't just a word; it's a guiding compass along their shared path.

Too often, couples get trapped in the allure of initial romantic feelings, mistaking infatuation for genuine love. Yet, true love is rooted in commitment—a conscious choice to love and cherish one another beyond the honeymoon phase, throughout every twist and turn life presents. It requires looking past immediate wants and focusing on the long-term health of the relationship. Commitment demands sacrifice, selflessness, and a willingness to grow together.

Commitment in a relationship is not just a checkbox to tick; it's a vibrant, living promise that requires our active participation every day. Imagine it as a beautiful garden—it thrives on love, nurtured by our conscious decisions to foster intimacy and support each other's growth. It's about creating a sanctuary where both partners feel treasured, respected, and valued, where love flourishes in an environment of open, honest communication.

Think of your commitment as an ongoing journey, marked not just by the vows exchanged on your wedding day, but by the countless small acts of love and kindness that weave the fabric of your partnership. Picture the quiet moments you share during a prayer, the laughter that rings through your home, and the unwavering support during life's storms. Commitment is also about granting forgiveness when mistakes happen, finding common ground in tough decisions, and continually striving to understand each other's hopes and dreams.

This journey is built on mutual respect, recognizing the unique gifts each partner brings to the relationship. It's not about one person leading the way; it's about collaboration and partnership. Imagine a space where both of you feel safe, cherished, and fully loved—a space that invites vulnerability. Sharing your deepest fears and greatest aspirations strengthens the bond between you and deepens your connection.

Your marriage is not just a shared journey; it's a testament to your faith in a higher plan. It reflects your trust in something greater that guides you through thick and thin. This divine partnership adds layers of meaning, making your commitment not just a human endeavor but a sacred bond. As you face challenges together and celebrate victories, you'll find that this commitment, fueled by faith and unwavering dedication, creates a relationship that grows stronger over time.

In the end, it's a promise that lasts beyond today—it's a vow for eternity, rooted in love and bound by faith. Embrace the beauty of this commitment; the power of your bond lies in the everyday moments that bring you closer and nurture your love for a lifetime.

A Promise of God's Presence

The unwavering commitment we explored earlier serves as the bedrock of a thriving marriage, yet it's only through the continual presence of God that this foundation can truly flourish. Think about it: a strong marriage isn't just about steadfast vows—it's about actively inviting God into the relationship, making His presence the lifeblood that nourishes it. Picture a majestic oak tree, its roots deeply embedded in the earth. The roots symbolize your commitment, while the sturdy trunk represents the marriage itself. But what about the sun, rain, and fertile soil? These are the elements that embody God's active presence in your life together. Without them, even the sturdiest tree will eventually wither.

God's presence in marriage isn't some distant ideal; it's a tangible, living reality that offers strength, comfort, and guidance. Imagine that gentle whisper you hear in moments of doubt or the unwavering support you feel during tough times. It's the boundless joy that lifts your spirits, often showing up in surprising ways—be it the subtle nudges from the Holy Ghost or the profound moments of answered prayer. Maybe it's the unexpected peace that blankets you and your partner during a conflict or the sudden clarity that cuts through confusion. These moments aren't just random; they signal God actively working in your lives, reigniting your connection and purpose.

Now, let's not forget the storms that life inevitably sends your way. Disagreements, financial struggles, health crises, the loss of loved ones—these challenges can really test even the strongest bonds. But during these turbulent moments, God's presence becomes a refuge, offering solace and a haven of peace amid the chaos. It gives you a perspective that exceeds the immediate troubles, reminding both of you that you are never alone. God's love envelops you, and His grace proves sufficient through every trial. It's during these vulnerable times that your faith can deepen, weaving tighter the bond not just between you and your spouse, but also with God.

And let's talk about prayer. This isn't just a ritual; it's an intimate conversation with the Divine, a lifeline connecting you both to God. Through prayer, you can voice your deepest hopes, fears, joys, and concerns. You can seek guidance in resolving those inevitable conflicts, ask for strength to overcome hurdles, and express gratitude for the blessings in your lives. Joint prayer becomes a powerful experience—one that cultivates unity and interdependence. It transforms challenges into opportunities for spiritual growth and deepens your intimacy. It turns your shared journey into a sacred space where you both can feel God's presence as a unified force in your lives.

The Bible is brimming with examples of God's active presence in relationships. Take Ruth and Boaz, for instance; their love story is steeped in faith and trust in God's providence. Or consider Abraham and Sarah, who remained steadfast despite facing significant obstacles. These narratives remind us that God's presence shines most brightly during trials and tribulations—not just during moments of comfort. These biblical couples didn't rely solely on their own strength but flourished through their faith in God's unwavering love and guidance.

Imagine a relationship where every argument is not a battleground but a stepping stone toward deeper understanding. That's the beauty of inviting God's presence into your marriage. When disagreements surface, it's all too easy to get caught up in blame and resentment. But when couples embrace God's presence, they can approach these challenges with humility and empathy. Picture this: instead of defensiveness, there's a genuine effort to listen and understand each other's feelings. With God gently guiding, couples can transform conflict into opportunities for growth, allowing their love to flourish.

Now let's talk about intimacy. This isn't just about physical closeness; it's a sacred gift that mirrors the divine love God has for us. Within God's presence, intimacy transcends the physical realm, turning into a spiritual communion that celebrates the bond between two souls. It's more than a moment of pleasure; it becomes an expression of unwavering love and devotion—a beautiful act of worship.

But the promise of God's presence doesn't stop at the two of you. It radiates outward, touching your family, friends, and community. When couples consciously seek God, their capacity for love expands, positively affecting everyone around them. Imagine being that beacon of hope, inspiring your children and neighbors, and strengthening your faith community. This outward expression of

God's love not only nurtures those connections but also deepens your own spiritual journey—a heartwarming cycle of growth and connection.

God is not a distant observer; He is actively involved in the journey of your marriage. Think about how His guidance manifests in small, everyday moments as well as in the miraculous—those times when you feel a nudge in the right direction or find unexpected solutions to challenges. By inviting Him along for the ride, couples find that He becomes a faithful companion, cheering them on through every hurdle and every milestone.

And here's the thing: seeking God's presence is not a one-and-done deal. It's an ongoing journey, full of daily commitments to prayer, Bible study, and worship. It's about being open to the gentle nudges of the Holy Ghost and trusting in His plan for your lives together. Each day is an opportunity to deepen your intimacy with God and with one another—a continuous path of spiritual growth that never ends.

In conclusion, the promise of God in marriage is a rich tapestry woven with strength, love, and guidance. It offers comfort in sorrow, joy in celebration, and wisdom amid uncertainty. Imagine transforming everyday challenges into growth opportunities and mundane moments into sacred experiences of faith. By actively nurturing this divine presence, couples can create a marriage that reflects the true power of God's love. It's a relationship built on unwavering faith, standing firm like a rock—worthy of every effort and every prayer. This is not just a partnership; it's a beautiful, thriving journey centered on a God who is ever-present and always loving.

Growing in Love and Grace

Imagine a garden, lush and vibrant, thriving because it receives constant care and attention. This lovely analogy perfectly captures the essence of a God-centered marriage, where commitment and the divine presence require continuous nurturing. Just like that garden, a marriage flourishes through consistent effort, growing in love, grace, and understanding—a dynamic, evolving journey that deepens intimacy with God and with one another.

At the heart of this growth lies the willingness to embrace continuous learning. Think about it: marriage is a whirlwind of experiences, challenges, and opportunities that demand our growth. We are not the same people we were at the altar; we are ever-evolving, learning, and adapting. This evolution invites us to acknowledge that we don't have all the answers—humility is key. Recognizing our flaws and remaining open to learning from mistakes is vital to nurturing our bond.

So, how can we continuously learn together? It might mean diving into regular Bible studies, deepening our understanding of God's word as it applies to our journey as a couple. Or perhaps it involves attending enriching retreats and workshops where we can gain practical skills for effective communication, conflict resolution, and intimacy. Seeking guidance from a therapist with a Christian perspective can also provide valuable insights, helping us navigate life's challenges. Ultimately, the commitment to grow—pursuing knowledge and wisdom together—enriches our marriage tremendously.

Equally important is the concept of grace—a beautiful, transformative force in our relationship. Grace means extending love and forgiveness, even when our spouse falls short. We must remember that we all make mistakes; we are all imperfect beings striving to please God. Offering grace doesn't condone wrongdoing; rather, it recognizes the power of forgiveness and the mercy we receive from God.

This doesn't mean ignoring unhealthy behaviors or compromising our well-being. Grace, within a healthy marriage, involves addressing failings with understanding while also setting boundaries and seeking help when necessary. It's about showing compassion, even in tough times, recognizing that our partners are grappling with their own challenges. As we navigate this path, seeking God's guidance will allow us to determine how best to offer grace and support one another.

Mutual understanding is another cornerstone of growth in marriage. Living together is merely the beginning; we must aspire to truly know and understand each other's hearts, dreams, fears, and hopes. This takes open and honest communication, active listening, and a willingness to empathize with our spouse's perspective—even when we disagree. It's about stepping into their shoes and deeply connecting with their emotions and spiritual journeys.

To foster this mutual understanding, we need to carve out time for meaningful conversations—moments devoid of distractions and interruptions. Regular date nights, shared hobbies, or even quiet evenings spent talking can create that space for connection. When we listen actively, we move beyond waiting for our turn to speak; we seek to understand first. Open communication, especially around challenging topics, helps create a safe environment where both partners feel valued and heard.

Additionally, recognizing and celebrating each other's strengths makes this journey even more rewarding. Marriage isn't a competition; it's a partnership built on mutual support and encouragement. By celebrating successes and offering support during tough times, we strengthen our bond, creating a safe space where both partners feel appreciated. This mutual appreciation builds security and solidifies the very foundation of our marriage.

In this beautiful journey of growth, we are called to cultivate not only our relationship with each other but also our connection with God, creating a thriving marriage filled with love, grace, and mutual understanding. So let's take this journey together, hand in hand, continually growing and blooming as we navigate the seasons of life.

Growing together as a couple is an incredible journey, but let's not forget the importance of blossoming as individuals, too. Personal growth is essential, and it's not just a nice-to-have—it's a game-changer! Imagine diving into personal prayer, immersing yourself in Bible study, and seizing opportunities for spiritual enrichment. Every step we take individually in our faith not only enriches our own spirits but also brings newfound depth to our marriage, forging a stronger connection with God and one another. It's about chasing spiritual maturity, which ultimately fortifies our relationship.

The rewards of this ongoing growth are priceless. We're talking about a deeper, richer marriage that can weather life's storms. This journey fosters intimacy—both emotional and physical—as we nurture understanding and trust. Instead of letting disagreements drive us apart, we transform them into stepping stones for growth and connection.

Of course, this journey isn't without its bumps in the road. We all face moments of doubt, frustration, and despair. But it's in these challenging times that our faith truly shines. When we lean on each other, seek God's guidance, and pray together, we can navigate adversity and emerge even stronger than before.

Ultimately, this journey of growing in love, grace, and mutual understanding is a lifelong commitment—a beautiful testament to our devotion to both God and each other. It's not about reaching a final destination; it's about embracing the process of continuous sanctification. With humility, grace, and a willingness to learn, we have the power to cultivate a marriage that resonates with the enduring love of God—a relationship that not only survives but truly thrives.

As we embrace this ongoing growth, we reflect the boundless love that God has for us. Yes, the path may not always be easy, but the treasures we uncover along the way far exceed the challenges we face. Life is a journey of faith, one that promises eternal blessings. The real beauty is not found in perfection but in our unwavering commitment to walk this path together, hand in hand, guided by the grace of God. Let's celebrate every step of this incredible journey!

Building a Legacy of Love and Faith

Building a lasting legacy is so much more than simply leaving material possessions behind; it's about etching an enduring mark on the hearts and minds of those who will come after us. For couples who are deeply rooted in faith, this legacy is a beautiful tapestry woven from threads of unwavering devotion, selfless love, and a life committed to serving God. It's a legacy that transcends our lifetimes, resonating through the generations, shaping their values, beliefs, and understanding of what it truly means to live a life that pleases God.

The journey to creating such a legacy begins with intentionally nurturing our own spiritual lives. This isn't a passive endeavor; it calls for conscious effort, daily dedication, and a fervent desire for a deeper intimacy with God. It's about setting aside precious time for personal prayer, Bible study, and moments of reflection. This isn't just a checklist; it's about cultivating a genuine relationship with God, allowing His presence to touch every corner of our lives. In those quiet moments of prayer and meditation, we unearth clarity, direction, and the strength necessary to tackle whatever challenges life presents. This personal connection with God lays the bedrock of a faith-filled life, establishing the foundation for a legacy that radiates His love.

However, building a legacy isn't done in isolation. Couples must actively create a shared spiritual journey. It means diving into regular Bible study together, engaging in thought-provoking discussions about theological concepts, and praying side by side. It's about being present in church services, joining small group ministries, and seeking out ways to serve the wider community together. These shared experiences not only strengthen spiritual bonds but also deepen the connection between spouses, fostering a unified understanding of their faith.

When we walk together on this spiritual path, our faith becomes a source of strength and unity—a treasure we can share and cherish. Think about it: the simple act of praying together, reading scriptures, and sharing life's ups and downs creates the bricks and mortar of a truly enduring legacy.

But wait, there's more! To truly inspire future generations, we must actively model the values and principles we wish to pass on. Living a life of integrity, honesty, and compassion isn't just a nice idea; it's essential. It means demonstrating forgiveness, grace, and understanding in our everyday interactions. It's about showing love and kindness not just to each other but to everyone we encounter. Our actions speak volumes; our children, grandchildren, and extended family will observe our lives and learn from our example. If we want our legacy to inspire faith, our lives must be a living testament to our beliefs. By consistently modeling faith-based values—like forgiveness, compassion, and unwavering commitment to God's word—we contribute to building the deepest, most lasting legacy possible.

Another key ingredient? Open and honest communication. We must cultivate a safe, supportive environment where family members are comfortable discussing their faith, their struggles, and their successes. Encouraging this open dialogue allows for the sharing of wisdom, the exploration of faith questions, and the strengthening of the family's spiritual foundation.

Sharing our faith stories—both the triumphs and the challenges—creates a rich tapestry of shared history and identity, becoming a powerful bond for future generations. By fostering this open and welcoming environment, we allow space for questions, doubts, and conversations that can guide younger generations on their own faith journeys.

Building a legacy of faith and love isn't just an obligation; it's one of life's most rewarding journeys. Imagine the laughter shared over family meals, the stories told during cozy nights by the fire, and the bonds strengthened through shared experiences. These moments cultivate a sense of belonging—an anchor in a world that often feels chaotic. Celebrating milestones together and supporting one another through life's challenges not only creates cherished memories but also reinforces the foundation of unconditional love that holds families together. This tapestry of relationships weaves a rich legacy that transcends mere belief; it's about nurturing the love and unity that define our lives.

Think about the larger community that surrounds us and the opportunities we have to make a real difference. When we step outside our front doors and engage with those around us—whether through volunteering, lending a helping hand, or simply offering a listening ear—we not only share our gifts but also embody the essence of faith in action. It's in these moments of service that our legacy expands beyond our families, shaping the world with compassion and care. Every act of kindness leaves a mark, establishing a legacy that our children and grandchildren can be proud of and aspire to continue.

Mentorship is another powerful way to build a lasting legacy. Have you ever considered how your life experiences could guide the next generation? By investing time in mentoring young people—whether through casual conversations or structured guidance—we can pass on our wisdom and help them navigate their own spiritual journeys. This exchange isn't just about teaching; it creates a vibrant chain of faith that ignites passion and purpose in others, ensuring that the light of our collective beliefs shines brightly through the years.

And let's not forget the power of the written word. Imagine penning letters to future generations, sharing stories and insights from your spiritual journey. Documenting our experiences, whether through journaling or writing a family history, can serve as a beacon of hope and inspiration for those who follow in our footsteps. These written legacies provide a tangible connection to our values and beliefs, allowing future family members to explore their heritage and understand the faith that shaped their ancestors.

As we embark on this journey of legacy-building, it's essential to remember that it is not a destination but a continuous adventure filled with growth, learning, and refinement. There will undoubtedly be moments of doubt and difficulty along the way, but it's through our perseverance and unwavering commitment to faith that we can create something truly beautiful. Each imperfection and challenge we face only adds depth to our story, showcasing the real, gritty journey of faith and love.

Ultimately, the legacy we leave behind isn't measured by material wealth or accolades. It's defined by the love we nurture, the faith we embody, and the positive impact we have on the lives around us. Just picture the ripple effect of God's grace as it weaves through our lives, shaping the hearts of our children and inspiring generations to come. By embracing this journey with intentionality and an open heart, we can leave a lasting legacy—a testament to the incredible power of faith and love that resonates through the ages. So, let's embark on this adventure together, crafting a legacy that reflects the beauty of our shared journey and the unyielding strength of God's love.

A Lasting Covenant with God and Each Other

The journey of faith, as we've explored, isn't a sprint; it's a marathon—a lifelong commitment that requires unwavering dedication and steadfast reliance on God's grace. This covenant, this sacred agreement we make with God and with each other, isn't etched in stone but rather woven into the very fabric of our lives. It is strengthened by each passing day, each shared prayer, and each act of selfless love. It stands as a testament to the enduring power of love that transcends the earthly realm, anchored in the unwavering faithfulness of God.

Think of it like a vine, delicately planted and in need of constant nurturing and care. In the beginning, it's a slender shoot, easily swayed by the winds of adversity. However, with consistent watering—through our daily devotionals, shared prayers, and intentional acts of love—it takes root, grows stronger, and ultimately becomes a mighty vine capable of withstanding even the fiercest storms. The storms will come, inevitably.

Disagreements, challenges, and life's inevitable trials will test the strength of our covenant. Yet it is in these moments of adversity that the true strength of our commitment is revealed. Our ability to navigate these storms together, leaning on each other and on our faith, deepens and strengthens our covenant.

This covenant is not merely a promise; it is a living, breathing entity, constantly evolving and expanding as we grow in our understanding of God and our love for one another. It is a journey of continuous learning, forgiveness, and reconciliation. It requires a willingness to set aside our pride, acknowledge our flaws, and seek forgiveness when we fall short. It's about recognizing that we are human, fallible beings, bound together by a love that is both human and divine. The imperfections, stumbles, and moments of doubt are not signs of failure; rather, they are opportunities for growth, for deepening our understanding of grace, and for strengthening our bond with God and each other.

One of the critical aspects of maintaining a lasting covenant is consistent, open communication. This goes beyond merely exchanging pleasantries or recounting the day's events; it involves sharing our hearts, fears, hopes, and dreams with one another. We must create a safe space where vulnerability is seen as a strength rather than a weakness, and where honesty is valued above all. This requires active listening and a willingness to understand each other's perspectives, even when those perspectives differ. It's about meeting each other where we are, acknowledging the emotional landscapes of each other's lives, and offering understanding and compassion. The focus should be on accepting each other unconditionally, flaws and all, just as God accepts us.

Another vital element is prayer—a constant, ongoing dialogue with God, not just as individuals but as a united front. Prayer isn't a magical formula; it is an act of surrender and an acknowledgment of our dependence on God's grace and guidance. Through prayer, we seek His wisdom, strength, and peace. We present our challenges to Him, trusting in His unwavering love and His ability to guide us through even the darkest times. Praying together, sharing our joys and sorrows, and expressing our hopes and fears creates a unique sense of unity and intimacy, drawing us closer to one another and to God. It becomes a shared space of vulnerability, reflecting our covenant with God and each other.

The foundation of our covenant rests on forgiveness—a willingness to extend grace, let go of past hurts and resentments, and embrace the healing power of God's love. Forgiveness does not mean condoning wrongdoing; it is about releasing the burden of anger and bitterness that can poison a relationship and hinder spiritual growth. It is an act of faith, trusting in God's ability to restore and heal. Holding onto anger and resentment hurts us; forgiving each other and ourselves sets us free and allows us to build a stronger, more resilient relationship. Forgiveness is as much an act of self-care as it is an act of love for our partner. It requires humility and a willingness to acknowledge our own imperfections, recognizing our need for God's grace and mercy.

Mutual support is essential in maintaining this sacred bond. It involves celebrating each other's successes, offering encouragement during difficult times, and providing steadfast support in pursuing personal goals. This kind of partnership requires active participation in each other's lives and demands empathy and understanding, even when we don't fully grasp the challenges each other faces. It's about creating a relationship where both individuals feel valued, appreciated, and unconditionally loved. This system of mutual support strengthens our ability to navigate life's complexities and builds a resilient foundation for our relationship.

The covenant also calls for a commitment to continuous personal growth. This means actively engaging in spiritual disciplines such as Bible study, prayer, meditation, and service to others. It's about striving to become more Christ-like, deepening our understanding of God's word, and living out our faith in meaningful ways. This personal growth not only enhances our individual faith but also enriches our relationship, fostering mutual respect and admiration.

It provides common ground for spiritual discussions, facilitates shared growth, and encourages a deeper understanding of each other's spiritual journeys.

This journey of faith—this ongoing covenant with God and each other—is not without its challenges. There will be moments of doubt when we question our faith and times when the weight of our struggles feels almost unbearable. However, it is in these moments that the true strength of our covenant is revealed. Through perseverance and unwavering faith, we emerge stronger, our bond deepened by the trials we have overcome together. The journey itself becomes a testament to the resilience of our faith and the unwavering nature of our commitment. It's a shared tapestry woven with threads of joy, sorrow, triumph, and struggle—a masterpiece that reflects the beauty and complexity of a God-centered life.

The key is to remember that this covenant is a partnership, a journey undertaken together, with God as our guide and our unwavering faith as our compass. It involves supporting, celebrating, and growing in love and faith together. Embracing imperfections, learning from mistakes, and continually seeking forgiveness from both God and each other are essential aspects of this journey. It is a lifelong commitment, a testament to the power of love, grace, and unwavering faith in a God who is ever faithful and always present.

This journey is defined by faith, not by a final destination. As long as we remain committed to this covenant, we will find strength, peace, and abiding love in God's embrace and in each other's. This is the lasting legacy we strive to create—a legacy of faith, love, and unwavering devotion, passed down through generations and serving as a beacon of hope in a world that desperately needs it. As we continue this journey, we must always remember that the covenant, the bond, and the love we share are far greater than any individual trial. In our enduring commitment, we find strength and hope.

Our lives form a tapestry, interwoven with the threads of faith, love, and forgiveness, which becomes a testament to the enduring power of a God-centered marriage. It's not a perfect picture but a beautiful mosaic; its imperfections add to its unique charm and authenticity. This journey reflects our growth, struggles, triumphs, and unwavering commitment to God and to each other. The journey is our legacy, shaped by the grace and mercy that have strengthened our relationship.

This legacy we leave behind is a living testament to the transformative power of a God-centered life and a love that transcends earthly boundaries. Our covenant is forever strengthened and reaffirmed, creating a bond that endures. It is a love that grows and a faith that shines brightly, illuminating the path for generations to come. This covenant embraces life's complexities, acknowledges human imperfections, and remains steadfast in its commitment to God and the love shared between two hearts bound by faith. In that commitment, we find the ultimate and enduring blessing—a life lived in love, faith, and service to God. This is a legacy that transcends time and continues to inspire.

My prayers are with you as you journey towards becoming God's duo and discovering the power of a God-centered marriage.

DISCUSSION QUESTIONS

Chapter 1

1. In what ways does the idea of "one flesh" reflect the spiritual significance of marriage beyond physical union?

2. How does Jesus' attendance at the wedding in Cana elevate the significance of marriage?

3. What do Ephesians 5:22-33 reveal about the roles of husbands and wives in a biblical marriage?

4. How is mutual submission characterized differently from dominance or control in a marriage context?

5. How does understanding each partner's strengths and weaknesses contribute to a healthier marriage?

Chapter 2

1. How can we better support each other's dreams and aspirations in our daily lives?

2. What are some specific ways we can pray for each other on a regular basis?

3. In what moments do you feel the most vulnerable in our relationship, and how can we create a safe space for sharing those feelings?

4. How can we integrate shared spiritual practices into our weekly routine to deepen our connection?

5. How do you feel we can improve our communication about personal challenges or spiritual struggles?

Chapter 3

1. What unique gifts or talents do you each bring to your shared mission?

2. What have been some of your most meaningful experiences serving others, either individually or as a couple?

3. How can you make your faith a more integral part of your daily lives as you pursue this mission together?

4. In what ways can you hold each other accountable to your goals while also providing encouragement and support?

5. What are the core values that guide your lives, and how can they inform your mission together?

Chapter 4

1. How can we better support each other in practicing the principles of love and forgiveness in our relationship?

2. What's one area of our lives where you feel we can apply biblical wisdom more intentionally?

3. How can we make our Bible study time more enjoyable and engaging for both of us?

4. What do you think is the most important aspect of nurturing our spiritual connection as a couple?

5. What questions do you have about the text we studied, and how can we explore them together?

Chapter 5

1. What specific ministries or volunteer opportunities within your church might you and your spouse be interested in joining together?

2. How do you think building friendships with other couples in your church can support your spiritual journey?

3. What unique talents or skills do you feel you can contribute to your church community?

4. What are some challenges you might face when trying to get more involved in your church, and how can you overcome them?

5. How can shared acts of service and compassion enhance your relationship with each other and with God?

Chapter 6

1. How does understanding God's unconditional love reshape our expectations of love within marriage?

2. What role does forgiveness play in a God-centered marriage, and how can it be practiced effectively?

3. Why is open and honest communication considered a vital aspect of a strong marital relationship?

4. How can recognizing and embracing one's own imperfections lead to greater compassion and understanding in a marriage?

5. How can engaging in shared prayer empower a couple to face life's challenges together?

Chapter 7

1. What steps can you take to address personal shortcomings and reflect Christ more effectively in your daily life?

2. How do you recognize pride manifesting in your marriage, and what strategies can you implement to combat it?

3. What role does humility play in fostering a healthy, loving relationship?

4. How can developing self-awareness improve communication and eliminate misunderstandings with your spouse?

5. How can you practice empathy and compassion in your relationship to foster a deeper connection?

Chapter 8

1. How can we intentionally model our faith to ensure our children absorb its values?

2. In what ways can we turn our mistakes into teaching moments for our kids?

3. How can we make Bible study engaging and relevant for children?

4. How can we create an environment of open communication where our children feel safe discussing their faith and struggles?

5. How can we approach discipline in a way that reinforces godly values without instilling fear?

Chapter 9

1. What does commitment mean to you in the context of your relationships, particularly in marriage?

2. In what ways can humility play a role in overcoming conflicts within a marriage?

3. What are some practical ways to stay committed during the challenging seasons of life?

4. What are some rituals or practices couples can adopt to strengthen their commitment over time?

5. How can recognizing the difference between infatuation and true love impact the longevity of a relationship?

6. In what ways can forgiveness be a cornerstone of a committed partnership?

7. How can you create an environment in your relationship where both partners feel cherished and valued?

8. What are some fears or aspirations that you would like to share with your partner to deepen your connection?

9. What challenges do you think most couples face in maintaining commitment, and how can they overcome these obstacles?

10. How does your commitment to your partner reflect your commitment to God, according to the beliefs expressed in the text?

Glossary

This glossary defines key terms used throughout the book to ensure clarity and understanding.

Covenant: A sacred agreement or promise, especially between God and humanity, or between husband and wife.

Spiritual Disciplines: Practices that foster spiritual growth and deepen one's relationship with God, such as prayer, Bible study, fasting, and meditation.

Grace: Unmerited favor or love from God.

Forgiveness: The act of releasing resentment and anger towards oneself or another.

Mutual Support: The act of providing encouragement, understanding, and assistance to one's spouse.

.

ACKNOWLEDGMENTS

To my families and friends, whose unwavering support and prayers have sustained me throughout this journey: Your love and encouragement have been a constant source of strength and inspiration.

A special thank you to Kiara Espinoza, Hannah Espinoza, and Brandie Fowler for their invaluable guidance and expertise in shaping this manuscript. I would also like to express my gratitude to Kevin Gaines, Preston Espinoza, Joseph Tomlin, and my grandbabies, Parker and Jazlyn Espinoza, for their understanding of the long hours involved in this process and for taking on extra responsibilities so that I could have the time needed to complete this work.

Above all, I want to thank God for His immeasurable grace, mercy, and unwavering love, which have been the foundation of our lives and the inspiration for this book.

ABOUT THE AUTHOR

Karen Pless Gaines has passionately devoted her life to the vibrant world of ministry, a journey that began in her childhood as a pastor's daughter. Growing up in a home infused with faith and service, she developed a profound understanding of spiritual life, which naturally led her to embrace a leadership role within the ministry.

Her journey is marked by rich experiences that unveil the intricate dance of balancing the demands of faith, family, and a fulfilling professional life. Each challenge has deepened her insights, allowing her to appreciate the beauty and complexity of this balance. With an unwavering commitment to serving God, Karen inspires and uplifts others, empowering them to lead lives overflowing with purpose and faith. Her mission is to guide individuals on their spiritual paths, encouraging them to build meaningful relationships with their families and communities that reflect the love and grace she embodies.

Karen is also passionately devoted to supporting women who are navigating the challenging transition out of abusive situations. Through her compassionate guidance, she creates a safe and nurturing environment where these women can rebuild their lives. Karen helps them discover their unique strengths and potential by fostering a sense of hope and self-worth. Drawing on the transformative teachings of Christ, she encourages them to embrace the possibilities of a brighter future filled with purpose and fulfillment, guiding them every step of the way toward a truly enriching life.